Succession Planning

Succession Planning

A Framework and Guidelines for School Leaders

Christopher M. Parfitt

ROWMAN & LITTLEFIELD
Lanham • Boulder • New York • London

Published by Rowman & Littlefield
An imprint of The Rowman & Littlefield Publishing Group, Inc.
4501 Forbes Boulevard, Suite 200, Lanham, Maryland 20706
www.rowman.com

86-90 Paul Street, London EC2A 4NE, United Kingdom

Copyright © 2023 by Christopher M. Parfitt

All figures created by author unless otherwise stated.

All rights reserved. No part of this book may be reproduced in any form or by any electronic or mechanical means, including information storage and retrieval systems, without written permission from the publisher, except by a reviewer who may quote passages in a review.

British Library Cataloguing in Publication Information Available

Library of Congress Cataloging-in-Publication Data

Names: Parfitt, Christopher M., 1982- author.
Title: Succession planning : a framework and guidelines for school leaders / Christopher M. Parfitt.
Description: Lanham, Maryland : Rowman & Littlefield Publishers, 2022. | Includes bibliographical references and index. | Summary: "A framework and practical guidelines for creating, implementing, and evaluating succession plans for any educational organization"—Provided by publisher.
Identifiers: LCCN 2022026114 (print) | LCCN 2022026115 (ebook) | ISBN 9781475860924 (cloth) | ISBN 9781475860931 (paperback) | ISBN 9781475860948 (epub)
Subjects: LCSH: Educational planning. | School administrators—Professional relationships.
Classification: LCC LB2806 .P354 2022 (print) | LCC LB2806 (ebook) | DDC 371.2/07—dc23/eng/20220718
LC record available at https://lccn.loc.gov/2022026114
LC ebook record available at https://lccn.loc.gov/2022026115

Cum ad aeternam memoriam—with eternal remembrance, I dedicate this volume to my godmother and aunt, Catherine L. Mongell (1963–2019). As my siblings and I were her succession plan, may her memory live on forever.

Contents

Foreword	ix
Preface	xi
Acknowledgments	xiii
Introduction	xv
Chapter 1: An Introduction to Succession Planning	1
Chapter 2: Basics of Talent Identification	11
Chapter 3: Multiple Measures of Talent	25
Chapter 4: Internal versus External Sources of Talent	33
Chapter 5: Characteristics of High-Potential Talent	43
Chapter 6: An Overview of Talent Management	53
Chapter 7: Avoiding Generic Training	61
Chapter 8: Targeted and Specific Development	71
Chapter 9: Mentoring	81
Chapter 10: Issues of Retention	89
Chapter 11: Practical Solutions for Retention	99
Chapter 12: The Importance of Culture for Retaining the Best	109
Chapter 13: Bringing a Plan to Fruition	119
Chapter 14: Assessing a Plan	129

Chapter 15: Final Thoughts	139
Index	147
About the Author	151

Foreword

Our school systems have continued to evolve and change, which has precipitated the need for new school leaders to emerge to face the challenges that exist in today's schools. Strategic school systems have prepared for these changes by engaging in deliberate school succession planning, a practice of finding, developing, and promoting talented individuals to be tomorrow's school leaders. Even prior to the challenges that existed before COVID-19 altered our school system, succession planning was a practice that proactive school districts were engaging with to find qualified leaders capable of leading our changing schools.

Past research on succession planning has focused on school districts that are large and/or urban, and present succession planning as something that only the "big boys" can do. This notion is completely untrue. Any school system, from the small school district in rural Oklahoma with 300 total students to the large 90,000 mega school district in Central Florida can benefit from targeted and deliberate succession planning. Yes, size can make more resources available to perform succession planning, but the skills and framework remain the same—with the goal to create new leaders capable of running our schools of tomorrow.

I have been fortunate to have been involved in large- and small-scale succession planning studies across 12 different states and 20 different school districts and have seen a few common elements in the systems that have been successful. For succession planning to work, school districts must be willing to commit resources—both financial and human capital—to the efforts on succession planning and have a short-term (1–5 years) and long-term plan in place. From these resources and strategic planning, a framework can then be created specifically that is applicable to the needs of the district.

Also, it is imperative to remember that many challenges can exist to even the best efforts toward school leader succession. School districts may over-certify aspiring administrators to the point where their pipeline and pool get too full; something that could then cause the highest potential candidates to look outside of their school district for leadership opportunities. It is also possible that not enough candidates are ready to step into leadership positions, causing positions to open sooner than expected and individuals to be selected for leadership positions who are not prepared for the challenges they will face, leading to burnout or self-selection out of the field. It should also be considered that districts may still seek external candidates to balance out their leadership pool, causing internal candidates to question their qualifications and credentials. All of these factors contribute to the underlying importance of having a system and framework in place before, during, and after deliberate and intentional succession planning.

Chris Parfitt has written a road map and guide to succession planning, calling upon previous experiences as a teacher, leader, administrator, and higher education practitioner to offer both small-scale and large-scale solutions to succession planning. Chris's book offers four parts, identification of leadership talent, development and mentoring, retention, and a summary with specific recommendations to assess succession planning. In particular, I was drawn to Chapter 5, "Characteristics of High-Potential Talent," as a unique take on succession planning that really hasn't been explored in much depth in educational literature. Chris addresses one of the biggest challenges with succession planning, when unqualified candidates get promoted for political reasons. This chapter also discusses quasi-leadership roles (deans, instructional coaches, curriculum specialists, and department chairs) that have generally been used as a way to prepare candidates for administrative positions. Equally important is whether or not an administrative candidate "fits" within the context of the school. A candidate may have all of the necessary criteria to be an administrator, but sometimes, intangibles related to culture, personal ties, and experiences mean more than credentials.

Chris's book is a great book for both scholars and practitioners alike. I can see his book being used by school districts looking to either develop or fine-tune a leadership pipeline, or higher education institutions looking to teach concepts of succession planning to future district-level administrators such as leadership directors or superintendents. I highly recommend Chris's book as a welcome piece of educational leadership literature for all interested in the field.

Lou L. Sabina, Ph.D.

Preface

Having researched succession planning in education for several years, I was constantly asked by professional colleagues, "when are you going to write a book?" This volume is the answer to the question. Feedback from peer reviewers from several of my articles was indication that the best practices I had been citing from business and medical literature were basically unknown to other educational researchers.

I wrote this book to document all I have learned on the topic and to frame as a usable and understandable guide to enact quality succession-planning processes in any educational organization—primarily primary and second schools and school districts, but the aspects are applicable to higher education settings with some modification. No two settings are the same, and so a deep understanding of organizational culture is vital. Hopefully, this book will be useful to anyone in a school leadership position to plan for continuity and ensure continued success.

Acknowledgments

There are so many individuals to thank for helping make this book a reality. Any errors or omissions are mine alone. Because all contributions were invaluable, names are listed alphabetically among groups. The entire team at Rowman & Littlefield has been stellar, with special thanks to Ms. Megan DeLancey, production editor, Ms. Kira Hall, assistant editor, Dr. Tom Koerner, vice president and executive acquisitions editor, and Ms. Carlie Wall, managing editor.

Thank you to those individuals who served as external reviewers; their feedback helped improve the book: Dr. John R. Jones, University of Oklahoma (now Southern Nazarene University); Dr. Brianne M. Lopez-Romano, Cape Coral Charter Schools; Dr. Jackie Mania, Education Partnerships; Dr. Amanda L. Rose, School District of Lee County (SDLC); and a special thank you to Dr. Lou L. Sabina, Stetson University, for reviewing and writing the foreword.

Thank you to my colleagues at Hodges University. Although there are too many fine individuals to name all, I wish to thank a few individuals with whom I worked the closest: Dr. Mahsa Alizadeh, Ms. Carol E. Ames, Mr. Byron "Skip" Camp, Ms. Tracey L. Durham, Dr. Anique A. Falconer, Dr. Afsaneh I. Farhadi, Ms. Petra B. Lopez, Ms. Karen A. Karavitis, Ms. Angela Manley, Dr. John D. Meyer, Ms. Melissa L. Mitro, Mr. Jesse R. Meyers, Ms. Lisa P. Osorio, Dr. Patricia H. Ottow, Ms. Erica M. Vogt, Ms. Victoria L. Walker, Ms. Riva G. Wharton, and Ms. Michelle D. Zamniak.

Thank you to my mentors and coauthors for their advice and input over many years: Dr. Cecil F. Carter, Florida Gulf Coast University (FGCU) Emeritus; Dr. Lynette C. Fields, School District of Pinellas County; Dr. W. Steve Lang, University of South Florida; Dr. LaSonya L. Moore, University of South Florida; Dr. Dorothy C. Rea, FGCU Emerita; Dr. Thomas C. Valesky, FGCU Emeritus; and Dr. Judy R. Wilkerson, FGCU.

Thank you to my board colleagues from the Southern Regional Council on Educational Administration: Dr. William A. Bergeron, University of

Alabama; Dr. Jason C. Bryant, Auburn University; Dr. Yvette P. Bynum, University of Alabama; Dr. Dana M. Griggs, Columbus State University; Dr. Dawn D. Guice, Louisiana Tech University; Dr. Jessica M. Hanna, Ohio State University; future Dr. Misty L. Henry, University of Oklahoma; Dr. Eugenia Lambert, Marshall University; Dr. Evan G. Mense, Southeastern Louisiana University; Dr. W. Art Rouse Jr., East Carolina University; and Dr. Ashley J. Wicker, Southeastern Louisiana University.

Thank you to former colleagues and graduate students for their input and perspectives on current school operations: Ms. Michelle R. Garafola, Collier County Public Schools (CCPS); Mr. Benjamin, Mrs. Loretta, Ms. Isabella, and Ms. Gabriella Goldenberg, Formerly Gateway Charter School; Dr. Danielle M. Hudzina, Charlotte County School District; Ms. Beverly King, SDLC retired; Dr. Kyle LaPaglia, CCPS; Ms. Karen J. Leonardi, SDLC retired; Ms. Nicole M. Micieli, CCPS; Ms. Maria Molano, SDLC; Ms. Lynette C. Rodriguez-Wibbels, SDLC; Ms. Sarah G. Rogozinski, Fairfax County Schools; Ms. Jennifer J. Shaffer, SDLC; Ms. Valerie E. Sheckler, SDLC; and Ms. Sarah N. Wallace, CCPS.

Finally, thanks to my family for everything! To my personal succession plan, my sons Alexander G. Parfitt, John C. Parfitt, and Luke R. Parfitt; to my parents, Debra A. Parfitt and Richard A. Parfitt; to my grandparents, Annetta M. Parfitt and Ronald L. Parfitt Sr., and Hisako Mongell and the late John S. Mongell; to my sister, Shannon L. Esdale, her husband Paul W. Esdale, and my niece Charlotte C. Esdale; to my brother, Andrew R. Parfitt, his wife Erica L. Parfitt, my nephew Asher A. Parfitt, and my nephew, Jaxon H. Parfitt; and to my uncles, Edward Mongell, Ronald L. Parfitt Jr., Robert S. Parfitt, the late Randy S. Parfitt, and my cousins, thanks for everything!

Introduction

This book is divided into several sections based on the components of a quality succession plan. The concepts and terminology are introduced in Chapter 1. Chapters 2 through 5 are focused on identification of talent. Chapters 6 through 9 are focused on targeted and specific development and mentoring. The focus of chapters 10, 11, and 12 is retention of high-performing employees. Chapters 13, 14, and 15 are focused on the overarching view and assessment of succession plans.

Most chapters contain a checklist, guide, or short case study to illustrate the pertinent aspects from the chapter. My goal is to provide usable information that can be readily adopted to assist school leaders with best practices and procedures to identify the most promising talent, provide specific development and quality mentoring opportunities, and retain high-performing talent.

Chapter 1

An Introduction to Succession Planning

Ask any person in a school setting to define succession planning, and the answers will be widely varied. In fact, many of those individuals will not be able to define succession planning succinctly. During an interview, an aspiring principal once stated, "[t]his is bad to admit, I had to look up to see what the term succession planning meant."[1] This aspiring principal is unfortunately not alone.

In fact, many school leaders are unfamiliar with the terminology and have been slow to embrace the concepts used by business leaders and managers in other fields for decades.[2] Unfortunately the lack of understanding and the unfamiliarity with the process and associated best practices have led to rapid turnover among school leaders[3] and far too many instances of an incorrect person being chosen for an important leadership position.

Is understanding the proper terminology enough to ensure success? Unfortunately no, but even educational researchers are often unfamiliar with best practices determined from other disciplines. The term *replacement planning* was once replete in the vernacular of top business executives. In its simplest form, replacement planning required a person to keep a chart with one (or more) individuals identified to replace a person in an executive position.[4]

However, replacement planning soon proved to be ineffective at handling the fluidity among business executive positions. John Beeson, a business author and national consultant, asserted that replacement planning had been proven to be obsolete by the 1990s.[5] Yet, as Francine Riddick[6] contended in her 2009 dissertation, educational leaders were very slow to adopt best practices from other enterprises. Riddick was correct because, a few years later, noted educational researchers recommended that school leaders begin to use replacement planning.[7]

DEFINING SUCCESSION PLANNING

As educators and others are often unfamiliar with the terminology, before initiatives can be assessed, programs created, or individuals prepared to succeed, succession planning must be defined. Although there are multiple definitions found in scholarly literature, a relatively simple definition is used in this book: succession planning is a comprehensive and systematic process by which individuals are prepared to assume positions of greater authority at *all* levels of an organization.[8]

The belief that succession planning must encompass all levels of the organization is important, as early succession planning literature focused exclusively on chief executive succession.[9] Although the literature on succession planning in schools is scant, previous works focused primarily on the school principal position.[10]

The succession-planning process itself can be viewed in three overlapping phases:

- Identification of high-potential leadership talent
- Targeted and specific development and mentoring
- Retention of high-performing employees[11]

To be successful for each phase and the entirety of the process, the unique and specific organizational culture must be considered.[12] Furthermore, to ensure success, there are other overlapping aspects that will be addressed in later chapters.

Having a common definition and understanding phases of the succession-planning process is still not enough to guarantee success. Specific actions are required of several individuals to guarantee success in the process. Perhaps the most prolific author on business succession planning, William Rothwell ascribed 15 characteristics evident in organizations with successful processes.

The most effective succession plans frequently contained all or most of these 15 characteristics: (a) participation of senior management, (b) benchmarks and needs assessments, (c) a developmental focus, (d) dedicated responsibility, (e) emphasis at all organizational levels, (f) a systematic approach, (g) analysis of future potential, (h) a timeframe for high-level replacement, (i) accountability to prepare successors, (j) specific training and development, (k) continual performance of current employees, (l) an understanding of the specific culture, (m) critical review of procedures, (n) focus beyond the next promotion, and (o) formal mentoring.[13]

Each of Rothwell's 15 characteristics are needed in one or more of the major components required for quality succession planning. Through the following chapters, specific, research-based processes, short case studies, and recommendations will be provided. Every organization, every school district, every individual school is different, and there is no "one-size-fits-all" solution, which is why understanding and framing a plan considering the unique organizational culture is crucial. "There is no silver bullet to school improvement, but the closest to a panacea in educational leadership is organizational culture."[14]

WHY THE FOCUS ON CULTURE?

Before answering why, what is culture must first be answered. Culture and the associated organizational climate have been well researched, and myriad definitions exist. For consistency, references to culture are framed through the definition provided by Robert Owens and Thomas Valesky; organizational culture is composed of the norms, values, and beliefs held by the individuals within the organization.[15] To understand an organization's culture, one must know the history, reveal the heroes and heroines, and acknowledge the rituals. Owens and Valesky view culture as one of the four major components to organizational climate. The others are ecology, milieu, and social systems.[16]

A lack of understanding about the unique organizational culture can be detrimental. Success at one level does not guarantee success at another. An excellent teacher may not be an acceptable curriculum specialist, a person who excels as a curriculum specialist may not be the appropriate person to become assistant principal, a high school assistant principal for discipline may not be the correct person to serve as an elementary principal, and so forth.

Yet, far too often, identification of talent is predicated on *current* job success. Rothwell described this phenomenon as talent appraisal, which has a narrow focus on assessment of past performance. Quality planning needs what he called *performance management* with a focus on all work aspects from the past and present, as well as considerations for future performance and the impact to the work environment.[17]

In his 1997 book on preparing executive-level talent, Morgan McCall literally described the phenomenon of viewing identified talent as having "the right stuff." Those individuals who had the right stuff were endowed with almost mythical properties, destined to become great leaders . . . except when some failed, to which the excuse was those individuals truly did not have the right stuff.[18]

An example of the desire to find those individuals with mythical skills can be shown through the recent focus of researchers and even news reporters[19] writing about the concept of "turnaround" leadership. A reporter who was covering a story on turnaround principals included assertions that those who were successful had a specific understanding of the school's unique culture. Principals who were successful in a turnaround setting were deliberate in their actions and very cognizant of the school culture and climate.[20]

The problem with turnaround leadership opportunities is often the very lack of cultural understanding. Removing a principal who was deemed successful in one setting and then transplanting him or her to an underperforming school with the expectation that he or she will quickly improve student performance because of past success is a fallacy. Andy Hargreaves and Dean Fink took issue with the rapid succession of principals more than a decade ago. Furthermore, they believed that a principal should be left in the position for a minimum of five years.[21] Although longevity is beneficial, Michael Fullan noted, from the very first day in a position of leadership, one must plan for his or her departure to ensure continuity and sustainability.[22]

SUSTAINABILITY NOW?

But, organizational culture is supposed to be the closest to a panacea, so why the focus on sustainability now? The most succinct way to explain is to use a business analogy describing the varying levels of a business making widgets. The assembly line workers are most concerned with the task at hand, physically creating the widgets. The foreman is concerned with keeping everyone on track to meet the weekly goals. The department manager is less concerned with day-to-day operations and is responsible for ensuring quarterly goals are met.

As individuals are promoted to positions of greater responsibility, the focus on planning for future activities becomes greater. Mid-level executives are often most concerned with ensuring yearly goals are met, while senior executives need to plan three to five years into the future, and the chief executive should be considering the possibility for five or more years into the future.[23]

The same is true with a school setting. Although weekly or monthly plans should be produced in advance, the concern for most classroom teachers is the instruction and classroom management for the day at hand. Not all teachers have the same level of competence and experience, as Amanda Rose detailed in her study pertaining to support for teachers with temporary certification, those individuals often struggle with the basic "survival" needs to get through each day.[24]

Therefore, the best school leaders have to plan to help those individuals become successful, which will take time. Just as the individuals in the business analogy had to plan further into the future as responsibility increased, so to do educational leaders. School principals must have strategic plans to address the next one to three years. Senior district leaders must be planning for three to five years, and superintendents must consider five or more years into the future.

With the rapid turnover of principals and superintendents, initiatives and goals cannot begin anew with each change of personnel. There must be continuity in plans and objectives, which can only occur through sustainability in leadership.[25] However, sustainability does not equal a maintenance of status quo. Linda Lee described three possibilities in leadership succession: (a) planned continuity, (b) planned discontinuity, and (c) unplanned transition.

Planned continuity should be used when the organization is making appropriate progress and the next leader needs to continue and build upon prior success. Planned discontinuity is needed when changes have to be made, often because progress is insufficient. Even though the new leader is given the task to make substantive changes, he or she has an appropriate phased transition into the position and has a deep understanding of the organization and the cultural aspects. Finally, unplanned change is the worst, because there is no consideration for the change and no guarantee of continuity or positive change. To a great extent, leadership succession in schools is unplanned.[26]

In essence, a quality succession plan is not written and enacted for today or necessarily tomorrow, but to ensure the organization has the appropriate leaders and quality pool of future leaders almost indefinitely.[27] Thus, sustainability in leadership is key, which in turn requires an intimate understanding of the unique organizational culture and subcultures. The most important reason, school leaders have a significant impact on student learning. In their oft-cited book, Marzano, Waters, and McNulty ascribed a .25 effect size to the impact of a school principal on student learning. The effect was only second to the impact from the classroom teacher. Undoubtedly, having the wrong school leader can drastically affect student learning.[28]

WHAT NEXT?

The components of succession planning have been defined, the characteristics of successful organizations have been briefly discussed, and the importance of culture and sustainability have been established. Now what? Well, depending upon the position one occupies in an educational organization, the answer will be very different.

A superintendent who needs to ensure there are trained individuals ready to serve as assistant superintendent or senior directors will have different needs from a middle school principal, who will have different needs from an aspiring leader. The goal of this book is to provide a framework and guidelines to assist school leaders at all levels to assess current initiatives, create an effective succession plan, and establish the cultural shift needed to ensure effective plans become embedded into the organizational practices.

Although the goal is to provide a framework for organizational leaders, individuals can benefit by understanding the research-based, best practices and self-advocating for inclusion of these practices, and also by identifying their own areas for development and seeking appropriate mentors. Change often begins with one individual at a time.

To begin the process of identifying a successful and comprehensive plan, some guiding questions are listed in Figure 1.1. If the answers are all *no*, there is no need to panic. Even if answers are mostly *yes*, greater in-depth analysis of the plan and actions are needed.

JUST A STARTING POINT

The checklist in Figure 1.1 is only intended to serve as a rudimentary formative assessment to determine if a succession plan is written and available, was created with appropriate input, and considersproper talent identification, specific development, and retention of high-performing employees. Through the remaining chapters, greater details will be provided for effective processes to identify aspiring leaders with high potential, create plans to address specific development and mentoring opportunities, and determine if individuals with the greatest potential are remaining with the organization.

CONCLUDING THOUGHTS

Although the remaining chapters are structured in a linear approach (i.e., identifying, developing, and then retaining individuals), in providing an outline for success, a quality succession plan will be recursive and cyclical. A succession plan should not be "chiseled into granite," nor limited to identifying a few specific individuals. The goal is to have a quality pool of candidates at every level prepared to assume positions of greater authority.[29]

The focus in chapters 2 through 5 is to identify leadership talent, identify pitfalls typically seen in educational organizations, and provide specific research-based recommendations. Topics include (a) "Basics of Talent Identification," (b) "Multiple Measures of Talent," (c) "Internal versus External Sources of Talent," and (d) "Characteristics of High-Potential Talent."

The focus for chapters 6 through 9 includes processes for development and mentoring along with specific recommendations, including (a) "An Overview of Talent Management," (b) "Avoiding Generic Training," (c) "Targeted and

Does my school district (or individual school) have a written succession plan?

       [ ] *Yes*   [ ] *No*

Is the plan available for review by anyone?

       [ ] *Yes*   [ ] *No*

Was the plan created with input from all appropriate stakeholders?

       [ ] *Yes*   [ ] *No*

Is the written plan updated annually or sooner?

       [ ] *Yes*   [ ] *No*

To identify future leaders, do my school district leaders consider input from teachers, parents, and knowledgeable partners, not just a principal and higher-level administrators?

       [ ] *Yes*   [ ] *No*

For aspiring leaders, is individualized training provided, not just generic leadership development for all participants?

       [ ] *Yes*   [ ] *No*

Do promising aspiring leaders want to stay with the school district?

       [ ] *Yes*   [ ] *No*

Is there evidence of promising aspiring leaders actually staying in the school district?

       [ ] *Yes*   [ ] *No*

Figure 1.1. Basic Succession-Planning Checklist

Specific Development," and (d) "Mentoring." Mentoring includes aspects of peer-mentoring, informal, and established formal programs.

In chapters 10, 11, and 12, the focus includes aspects of retention and provide solutions and address cultural components for success. Topics include "Issues of Retention," "Practical Solutions for Retention," and "The Importance of Culture for Retaining the Best." Retaining high-performing candidates is vital for ensuring a pool of qualified individuals who are prepared to assume positions of greater authority.

Finally, in chapters 13, 14, and 15, the overarching and connected aspects to "bring everything together" is addressed, as well as specific recommendations on methods to assess succession planning. Practical advice and case studies are provided.

CHAPTER REFERENCES

1. Parfitt, C. M. (2017). Perceptions of succession planning in four Florida school districts: A mixed-method study. *Southeast Journal of Educational Administration, 17*(2), 88–115.

2. Riddick, F. P. (2009). *What is your bench strength? An exploration of succession planning in three large school districts in a southeastern state* (Publication No. 3360378) [Doctoral dissertation, North Carolina State University]. ProQuest Dissertations and Theses Global.

3. Hargreaves, A., & Fink, D. (2006). *Sustainable leadership*. Jossey-Bass.

4. Conger, J. A., & Fulmer, R. M. (2003). Developing your leadership pipeline. *Harvard Business Review, 81*(12), 76–84.

5. Beeson, J. (2000). Succession planning: Leading-edge practices: What the best companies are doing. *Across the Board, 37*(2), 38–41.

6. *ibid.*—Riddick (2009)

7. Zepeda, S. J., Bengtson, E., & Parylo, O. (2012). Examining the planning and management of principal succession. *Journal of Educational Administration, 50*(2), 136–158. https://doi.org/10.1108/09578231211210512

8. Chavez, J. (2011). The case for succession planning. *Strategic Finance, 92*(8), 15–16.

9. Zaich, L. L. (1986). *Executive succession planning in select financial institutions* (Publication No. 8612669) [Doctoral dissertation, Pepperdine University]. ProQuest Dissertations and Theses Global.

10. Hart, A. W. (1996). *Principal succession: Establishing leadership in schools*. SUNY Press.

11. *ibid.*—Chavez (2011)

Griffith, M. B. (2012). Effective succession planning in nursing: A review of the literature. *Journal of Nursing Management, 20*(7), 900–911. https://doi.org/10.1111/j.1365-2834.2012.01418.x

12. Parfitt, C. M. (2017). Creating a succession-planning instrument for educational leadership. *Education Leadership Review*, *18*(1), 21–36. https://www.icpel.org/uploads/1/5/6/2/15622000/elr_volume_18_number_1_fall_2017.pdf

13. Rothwell, W. J. (2005). *Effective succession planning: Ensuring leadership continuity and building talent from within* (3rdrd ed.). AMACOM.

14. Attributed to Cecil F. Carter, Ed.D., associate professor emeritus, Florida Gulf Coast University.

15. Owens, R. G., & Valesky, T. C. (2022). *Organizational behavior in education: Leadership and school reform* (12thth ed.). Pearson Education.

16. *ibid.*

17. *ibid.*—Rothwell (2005)

18. McCall, M. W., Jr. (1997). *High flyers: Developing the next generation of leaders*. Harvard Business School Press.

19. Bland, T. (2018, September 28). How does the Lee County School District turn around its failing schools? *Fort Myers News-Press*. https://www.news-press.com/story/news/education/2018/09/28/turnaround-principal-program-lee-county-school-district-failing-schools/925321002/

20. Lopez-Romano, B. M. (2020). *Turnaround principals' practices in the southeastern United States: A case study* (Publication No. 28412619) [Doctoral dissertation, University of West Florida]. ProQuest Dissertations and Theses Global.

21. *ibid.*—Hargreaves & Fink (2006)

22. Fullan, M. (2005). *Sustainable leadership*. Corwin Press.

23. *ibid.*—McCall (1997)

24. Rose, A. L. (2019). *Supporting alternative certification teachers' professional development needs in Florida: Knowledge of K–12 school leaders* (Publication No. 13808049) [Doctoral dissertation, Florida Gulf Coast University]. ProQuest Dissertations and Theses Global.

25. *ibid.*—Fullan (2005)

26. *ibid.*

27. *ibid.*—Conger & Fulmer (2003)

28. Marzano, R. J., Waters, T., & McNulty, B. A. (2005). *School leadership that works: From research to results*. Association for Supervision and Curriculum Development.

29. *ibid.*—Conger & Fulmer (2003)

Chapter 2

Basics of Talent Identification

Arguably, the most important phase in succession planning is the identification of high-quality talent. Without appropriate individuals prepared to assume positions of greater responsibility, no other aspect of succession planning matters. Whether from within the organization or external, being able to identify the individuals who have the knowledge, skills, and dispositions to be successful leaders is vital. The "stage is set" for a practical analysis of succession problems in Case Study 2.1 (in Figure 2.1), and then, throughout this chapter, an overview of the most appropriate research-based, best practices for identifying leadership talent is provided.

In educational settings, one of the most pervasive problems is the overreliance on processes directly contradictory to best practices.[1] As written in the first chapter, educational leaders are often unfamiliar with the concepts and best practices associated with succession planning; even worse, they often believe their current actions are effective.[2] For example, the worst possible metric for talent identification is the reliance on the singular recommendation from one direct supervisor.[3]

Yet, some in education have openly embraced the idea that the school principal should be the only person involved in identifying future school leaders.[4] Even when asked if perspectives of multiple individuals are used to identify future leaders, affirmative answers have to be viewed with the caveat that the multiple perspectives are generally limited to the principal and his or her direct supervisor.[5]

HOW TO IDENTIFY FUTURE TALENT

Relying on one supervisor's recommendation introduces emotional aspects to a subjective assessment. Candidates who do not have the greatest potential

Case Study 2.1

The New Superintendent's Oncoming Storm

You have just been appointed as superintendent of *Breeze City*, a small-town school district that also serves surrounding rural areas. The district contains one high school with approximately 2,000 students and 100 teachers; two junior high schools, each with approximately 1,200 students and 70 teachers; and eight elementary schools ranging in size from 500 students to 1,400 students. The culture at each school is very different.

Based on the most recent rankings determined from the state-mandated standardized tests, the district is performing well below the state average. Fewer than 70% of enrolled students graduate from high school and fewer than 40% of third-grade students are grade-level proficient in reading and fewer than 33% proficient in math. When asked about future ambitions, the most common answer from high school students is to be a professional athlete—the high school does not have a record of winning athletic teams.

Although there are relatively few teaching vacancies, over 50% of the teachers are related by marriage or generationally. The current high school principal is close to retirement and has been in the same position for over 15 years. His father was previously the high school principal. Among the central office administrative staff, the average age is 63; and, for all school-based administrators (including assistant principals), the average age is 58. Stability in leadership positions has not been a traditional problem; complacency has. Because of the lack of mobility, several well-respected teachers with great leadership potential have left the district to accept leadership roles in nearby locations.

The state department of education rules include a requirement for all school leaders to have graduated from an approved program at the master's-degree level or higher, as well as complete a district-sponsored leadership readiness program. There are few individuals with the requisite credentials in the organization. A previous administrator indicated the program only exists "on paper" to meet the state requirement. However, the nearest institution of higher education (a small primarily undergraduate-level state college) is located in an adjacent county over 40 miles away. The nearest major university is located almost 75 miles away. There has been little to no incentive for teachers to pursue advanced education in school leadership. Most of the surrounding school districts have similar issues.

You are the first superintendent hired from outside the school district in a generation. The members of the school board recognize that the lack of student achievement is not acceptable

> and with the aging leadership personnel, the school district is not prepared to replace most of the principals and central-office staff over the next 3 to 7 years.
>
> When consulting the senior leaders and head principals about potential leadership talent, frequent answers include: "I really like Joe's kid," "there are a few teachers at Eastside who have been with us for many years," or worse yet, "no one at my school seems interested in becoming a principal."
>
> The school board chair specifically stated that she expects a plan to improve student performance submitted to the board for approval within 60 days along with a revision of the five-year strategic plan, and for the superintendent's mid-year evaluation, a separate plan must be developed to identify and train individuals to become future principals.
>
> As superintendent, what do you do first? How will those future leaders be identified and by whom, what are the characteristics of good leaders, how to determine if the identified individual is the appropriate cultural fit for a specific position, and are processes developed to ensure there are individuals prepared for leadership positions in the future?

Figure 2.1. The New Superintendent's Oncoming Storm

may be rated highly because of a sense of personal loyalty and other non-job-related aspects.[6] Conversely, exceptional candidates may receive lower-than-deserved ratings because of jealousy or a perceived threat; or, fear of loss and a desire to keep a valuable employee in the same position.[7]

To mitigate the issue of subjective evaluations, an assessment involving multiple individuals is needed. The direct supervisor must be included; however, direct subordinates do as well. Individuals two levels above and below (if possible) need to be included, as do peers and qualified external individuals.[8] Senior leaders must also be active participants throughout the entire process.[9]

The process is often called a 360-degree assessment, which has purported origins from the German military during World War II, and with the earliest documented usage by Esso Research in the 1950s.[10] A person may "fool" one or two people, but the chance of fooling all of the assessors is rare. In addition, subjective factors from the direct supervisor will be minimized as other assessors will presumably not all have the same (positive or negative) emotional connections.

CONNECTIONS TO CULTURE

As mentioned in Chapter 1, the unique organizational culture must be considered during each phase and across the entire process. Consideration of culture is especially important when identifying future leaders. Whether internal or external, those individuals must be the proper fit for the organization. A person who does not share or honor the norms, values, and beliefs will not be successful over time, even if he or she was highly successful in a different setting.

One very important point of contention is the fact that a person is not necessarily the correct choice simply by virtue of being an internal candidate. Also, success at one level of the organization does not guarantee success at the next.

A board member for a large school district once evaluated a "homegrown" superintendent quite negatively. Although the individual had successfully "risen through the ranks," maintained support from certain members of the community, and obviously had strong connections to influential groups, the superintendent lacked the foresight to address future (and arguably current) needs. The board member described the superintendent's actions as "trying to run a multibillion-dollar enterprise like a 1950s mom-and-pop store." The description well highlights the importance for succession planning to address future organizational needs.

The aforementioned superintendent *may* have been a good principal or central-office employee. Unfortunately, this person was obviously not the correct person to be superintendent. Quite possibly, this individual's skill set would have been acceptable for the organization, but in the past. Rather than trying to recreate the "glory days" of old, the focus needed to be on creating the best days yet to come.

Although the school board member did not intend to do so, the individual highlighted an important point made by several authors,[11] identification of talent needs to be conducted considering the future organization needs, goals, and objectives. An analogy would be taking the family on a Hawaiian vacation; a pilot was needed to fly the plane, but upon landing in Honolulu, to get to the hotel, a taxi or shuttle driver is needed, not another pilot.

WHAT DOES THE FUTURE HOLD?

Assessing the needs of the future requires those in current positions to have vision and foresight. The general lack of future vision is highlighted well using the frequently cited Lewis Carroll quote from *Alice in Wonderland* in which Alice asks the Cheshire Cat for directions:

Alice: Would you tell me, please, which way I ought to go from here?

The Cheshire Cat: That depends a good deal on where you want to get to.

Alice: I don't much care where.

The Cheshire Cat: Then it doesn't much matter which way you go.[12]

Unless a specific destination is known, any movement will take one elsewhere. This is in fundamental disagreement with the concept of teaching future educators to be "change agents."

Around the beginning of the century, textbooks and articles were replete with righteous proclamations challenging future educators to become change agents.[13] The issue with the focus on change is the fact that change does not have an inherently positive (or negative) connotation. Change is just different, and without appropriate focus, change can be detrimental. When destructive behaviors become embedded into the culture, those negative behaviors are perpetuated by others and the cycle is difficult to stop;[14] therefore, positive change is not likely to occur.

The stakes are greater with an educational institution than a children's story, as initiatives by an individual who leads the organization in the wrong direction or fails to maintain adequate progress ultimately affects student learning negatively. As much as individuals, influential groups, and governmental entities want instant success, success takes time, especially when initiatives require a cultural or paradigm shift. Realistically, data are needed for three years to determine the impact of a curricular change, and the process should be viewed as continual, not a "snapshot" of progress.[15]

Regardless of having a grand vision or a substantial scope for new initiatives, an effective leader will not have success without the buy-in from the appropriate stakeholders.[16] Having a stellar vision does not matter if no one else supports it. Especially in an educational organization, having the requisite knowledge, skills, and dispositions is important for a leader.[17] Those attributes must translate into helping others in the organization grow. There are many reasons why authors of school leadership standards and leadership preparation program personnel include instructional leadership among the primary foci.

As John Jones and Misty Henry contended in several of their articles, helping teachers improve in all areas of instruction is a vital component of clinical supervision, which is one of the foremost responsibilities of an educational leader.[18] Therefore, identifying appropriate leadership candidates who have vision for the future is also not enough; each future leader must be able to assist others to improve.

CHARACTERISTICS OF HIGH-QUALITY CANDIDATES

As the need to identify those with vision, but also the knowledge, skills, and dispositions to assist others to grow, a fundamental question emerges, "what are the research-based characteristics of high-quality, high-potential candidates?" Morgan McCall literally described the long prevailing theory for executive talent as those who had the "right stuff."[19] Those predestined great ones were simply "born to lead." While the romanticized description might lend well to a movie trailer, as McCall later defined, the notion of simply having the right stuff is a myth. With each chapter, he added to the formula leading to having the right stuff and ultimately success.

In McCall's formula, experience, education, and setting all contributed to having the right stuff, which highlights the contention of the importance for considering organizational culture. So, are there truly universal characteristics evident in *all* great leaders, even just all great school leaders? No, but there are many characteristics frequently evident in a number of great leaders, and those traits can be identified and must be identified early.

Requisite knowledge and skills are a must; yet the greatest indicators are dispositions. In their books and numerous articles pertaining to dispositions, Judy Wilkerson and Steve Lang have consistently described dispositions as the values, attitudes, and beliefs held by an individual. Furthermore, dispositions can be assessed.[20] When assessing leadership dispositions, the determination is not whether the individual is correct or incorrect, right or wrong; the determination is simply to what extent do the answers align with specified standards.[21]

When teaching aspiring leadership students about dispositions, ask if they believe a person who hated children was a "bad" person. Inevitably, at least one student will say "yes." To which the appropriate response is that hating children is not illegal, not immoral, nor unethical. The response was simply information used to confirm that the person is not appropriate to teach kindergarten.

Most likely, a full battery of individualized dispositional assessments will not be used to assess every potential candidate, so what are some of the dispositions to identify in potential leadership candidates? Finance executive Jodi Chavez provided several generic characteristics of high-potential candidates: those individuals should have passion, integrity, and courage; have a vision yet be open minded; and be willing to take risks but also be able to learn from mistakes. Furthermore, those individuals must be trustworthy and have a clear sense of being value driven, while being humble and authentic.[22]

Because the assessment of dispositions is a determination to what extent the responses align to standards, and although some state departments of education use state-specific versions, a review of national standards is an appropriate starting point. The original 1996 version of the *Interstate School Leaders Licensure Consortium Standards for School Leaders* contained knowledge, skills, and dispositional statements.[23]

When the standards were revised in 2008,[24] a separate document contained the performance expectations, which included dispositional statements for educational leaders.[25] Although older versions, the dispositional statements still contain pertinent information for the desired attitudes, values, and beliefs of leadership candidates; the 2015 revisions in which the document was renamed the *Professional Standards for Educational Leaders* do not contain delineated dispositional statements, but rather contain embedded aspects within standards and indicators.[26] The best candidates demonstrate the knowledge, skills, and dispositions to be successful, but who are these individuals?

INTERNAL OR EXTERNAL SOURCES

"The expert is always somebody from out of town wearing a suit." While the adage does not reflect reality, unfortunately, there are those who believe the statement to be true. In a higher education setting, an institution had a renowned expert in a field in a high-level technical leadership position. After the expert left, the person in the deputy position assumed the vacated role on an interim basis.

After receiving promotional material from an external source, the supervisor asked the interim about bringing this consultant on campus to conduct trainings. The interim responded, "I have never heard of this person; we had the state's leading expert, whom we let walk out the door. Why would we pay to bring someone else here who knows less than the person we had?" The expression, "sometimes you don't know what you have got until it is gone" is apropos.

In a somewhat similar situation, a former student described an overwhelming process to be considered for a promotion as an internal candidate, despite the fact others applying for the position had substantially less experience and fewer academic credentials than her. After being selected for the promotion, a senior-level leader told her, "this is the last promotion you will ever receive here, so if you ever want more, then you will have to go elsewhere."

Unfortunately, those stories are not unique in educational organizations. There are always excuses purporting candidates need a specific experience or a different experience. The previous statements from senior leaders showed how little they were able to recognize talent within the organization. However, just as the previous discussion of the superintendent was a cautionary tale not to rely on the fact a person is an internal candidate, the same caution must be viewed when considering an external candidate.

So, there are problems with internal and external candidates? Yes! Inherently being an internal or external candidate does not make a candidate better or worse. Asking internal or external is the wrong question—is the person the proper organizational fit, and does he or she have the appropriate knowledge, skills, and dispositions to be successful now *and in the future*, are the proper questions. All aspects being equal is there a preference? Yes, and the subtitle to Rothwell's textbook provides an illuminating answer, "ensuring leadership continuity and building talent from within."[27]

Considering a candidate solely or weighted on internal compared to external status is a poor metric. However, an internal candidate identified as high performing, who knows the culture and was provided with substantial development opportunities and specific mentoring should be preferred to an external candidate. As business researchers Jay Conger and Robert Fulmer wrote in the early 2000s, senior leaders need to focus on development to ensure a consistent leadership pipeline is established for the organization.[28]

Once identified, the candidates need targeted and specific development and quality mentoring. Chapters 6 through 9 are dedicated entirely to developing leadership talent. Controlled development can only occur for internal candidates. Therefore, we must return to the question, how are those individuals identified?

MULTIPLE MEASURES OF TALENT

Earlier in the chapter, the importance of a 360-degree assessment and consideration of multiple viewpoints was mentioned. Chapter 3 is devoted entirely to multiple measures of talent; though, because of the importance, there is a need to reiterate. Destructive leadership practices are not always recognized as being destructive and, once embedded, are easily perpetuated.[29]

As found through prior research, leaders at all school levels often believed their actions were effective, and yet because of the unfamiliarity with best practices or even the terminology associated with succession planning, they were doing the exact opposite.[30] Even among case studies pertaining to succession planning in education, respondents typically provided anecdotal sources and platitudes for evidence of success, rarely—if ever—were empirically based results shown.[31]

Such anecdotal evidence included statements that the school principal is solely responsible for identifying future school leaders[32] or serving as an assistant principal is sufficient proof an individual will be an effective principal, simply because seven out of 10 interviewed principals indicated they were promoted within the same school.[33] In many of those settings, individuals followed the past precedence, completely unaware that the actions are contrary to best practices.

Not just in principles of succession planning, education as a field is typically slower to adopt aspects and processes from other disciplines.[34] To combat the trend, school leaders at all levels need to be exposed to best practices and research. The use of multirater assessments was adopted by many businesses well before the turn of the last century. Yet, another paradigm shift is needed to view high-performing talent as organizational-wide assets. Therefore, cross-functional assessments should be included.[35]

Defining the term *cross-functional* for educators can be difficult, as most are not familiar with the business vernacular. In simple terms, a leadership candidate who is a math teacher needs to be assessed by individuals who are not math teachers and on facets beyond the scope of teaching math or supervising other math teachers. To be an effective assistant principal, the candidate will need to assist English and science teachers to improve pedagogical practices. He or she will presumably handle student-discipline issues, present professional-development sessions, and possibly manage fiscal aspects. Being an effective math teacher does not guarantee success at the next level.

This is why Rothwell indicated a need to assess the person's capabilities beyond the next promotion.[36] Years ago, Ir was responsible for overseeing the employee recruitment process for a school district. During a recruitment event, I was stationed next to a team from a convenience store chain and had an opportunity to speak with those individuals. What was most interesting was their mind-set in hiring employees. The district manager for the chain said, "we don't look for someone who can run a cash register, we want someone with the skills to be managing a store in a year or two." Whether they realized or not, their viewpoint echoed authors who have stressed the importance of identifying future leaders while hiring for entry-level positions.[37]

To ensure continuity and appropriate succession management, senior leaders need to be involved with the process.[38] Assessments need to be conducted by a direct supervisor, his or her superordinate, any direct subordinates, subordinates two levels below, colleagues or peers, and knowledgeable external reviewers. While the process is not foolproof, a much greater assessment of potential will be made by using the 360-degree approach.[39]

EARLY DEVELOPMENT

Although identification, development, and retention are listed as three separate phases to succession planning, there is substantial overlap. While chapters 6 through 9 contain the full focus on development and mentoring, there are some overlapping aspects to address during the identification phase. Without having the appropriate developmental opportunities and experiences, having the knowledge, skills, and dispositions is not enough.

There is a reason that world-class athletes spend considerable time during the off-season to focus on strength training and conditioning. Describing the phenomenon, golf legend Gary Player once provided sage advice to a fan who indicated he would have given anything to hit a golf ball as well as Player. To the fan's surprise, Player responded:

> No, you wouldn't. You wouldn't be willing to do what it takes. You have to rise early in the morning and hit five hundred balls until your hands bleed. Then you stop, tape your hands, and hit five hundred more balls. The next morning you're out there again with hands so raw you can barely hold your club, but you do it all over again. If you do that through enough years of pain, then you can hit a ball like that.[40]

Without his intense training regimen, Gary Player would not have been as successful. The key to success was not just intensity but also duration; leadership development is very similar.

Those with the raw talent need opportunities to refine their skills continually. In business vernacular, opportunities to serve in an unfamiliar position are frequently referred to as "stretch assignments."[41] In a large-scale educational setting, removing a teacher from a classroom for an extended period of time to provide an opportunity to experience facets of an administrative job full time is generally not feasible. On a small scale, those opportunities can be provided and need to be facilitated for all identified candidates, not just for those currently pursuing a graduate degree.

CONCLUDING THOUGHTS

By its very human nature, personnel evaluations will have subjective elements. The only question is to what extent do those biases affect judgment? Therefore, processes should be defined to limit subjectivity to the maximum extent possible. Employing multiple raters is an aspect that must be stressed the most and is the focus for the entire next chapter in the book.

Case Study 2.1 Recommendations

The Superintendent's "Game Plan"

If I were the superintendent, the first step in creating a game plan toward creating a quality succession plan, would be to identify the characteristics and qualities needed for the position. Even the job descriptions may be outdated. By having a list of criteria—knowledge-, skill-, and disposition-based—will assist the assessors. Those criteria also need to be considered in relation to the strategic plans and goals. As I mentioned previously, the lists will not be static and should evolve as the organization grows.

Because the culture at each school is different, one team will not suffice. Teachers, support staff, parents, and even students should be involved in talent identification at the school level. The individuals in the positions closest to the superintendent should also be involved to a great extent, along with the principals and assistant principals.

Individuals with the knowledge, skills, and dispositions need to be encouraged to pursue graduate degrees in leadership. I would highly recommend working to establish a partnership with the nearest higher education leadership preparation program. With a minimum number of students, the university faculty might be willing to deliver courses at one of the schools using a cohort model. For longer term, formal partnerships can be created with neighboring school districts to increase the number of potential students in a cohort and increase the likelihood the university faculty would be willing to provide an on-site option.

A senior leader should be given the task to assess and reconstitute the district-based development program and ensure those who complete the program are ready to assume positions of increasing responsibility. Separate programs for aspiring assistant principals, principals, and central-office administrators are needed. Once identified, the development for all individuals needs to be targeted and specific.

By having a robust identification process and expansion of development opportunities at all levels, the superintendent can ensure a pipeline of qualified individuals is established. Once the processes are established and enacted, the superintendent and senior leadership can ensure that individuals are ready to assume the principalships and central-office positions in the near future, thus meeting the goal set by the school board chair.

Regardless of being internal or external, the candidate must have the requisite knowledge, skills, and dispositions, as well as share the norms, values, and beliefs of the individuals within the organization. The candidates *and those selecting them* must be visionary and forward thinking. By identifying promising talent early, developmental assignments can be leveraged.

Having defined the basic concepts of identification of talent, returning the focus to Case Study 2.1, general recommendations for the new superintendent for Breeze City are provided (see Figure 2.2). A quality succession plan must have input from appropriate stakeholders and consider the specific cultural aspects.

CHAPTER REFERENCES

1. Parfitt, C. M. (2017). Perceptions of succession planning in four Florida school districts: A mixed-method study. *Southeast Journal of Educational Administration*, *17*(2), 88–115.

2. Parfitt, C. M., Romano, B. M., Hudzina, D. M., & Rogozinski, S. G. (2020). Perceptions of leadership identification: A collective autoethnographical study. *Voices of Reform: Educational Research to Inform and Reform*, *3*(2), 82–95. https://doi.org/10.32623/3.10006

3. Beeson, J. (1998). Succession planning: Building the management corps. *Business Horizons*, *41*(5), 61–66.

4. Hengel, R. I. (2007). *Leadership capacity: Planning for leadership succession in schools* (Publication No. 304719536) [Master's thesis, Royal Roads University]. ProQuest Dissertations and Theses Global.

Steele, F. G. (2015). *Principal experiences of succession planning* (Publication No. 10012699) [Doctoral dissertation, Oklahoma State University]. ProQuest Dissertations and Theses Global.

5. *ibid.*—Parfitt (2017)
6. *ibid.*—Beeson (1998)
7. *ibid.*
8. *ibid.*

9. Rothwell, W. J. (2005). *Effective succession planning: Ensuring leadership continuity and building talent from within* (3rd ed.). AMACOM.

10. Thornton, S. (2017, July 5). *The history of 360-degree feedback.* https://careertrend.com/about-5163489-history-degree-feedback.html

11. e.g., *ibid.*—Beeson (1998)
ibid.—Rothwell (2005)

12. Carroll, L. (1865). *Alice's adventures in wonderland*. Macmillan.

13. e.g., Lane, S., Lacefield-Parachini, N., & Isken, J. (2003). Developing novice teachers as change agents: Student teacher placement "against the grain." *Teacher Education Quarterly*, *30*(2), 55–68.

14. Shaw, J. B., Erickson, A., & Harvey, M. (2011). A method for measuring destructive leadership and identifying types of destructive leaders in organizations. *Leadership Quarterly*, *22*(4), 575–590. https://doi.org/10.1016/j.leaqua.2011.05.001

15. Cordeiro, P. A., & Cunningham, W. G. (2013). *Educational leadership: A bridge to improved practice* (5th ed.). Pearson Education.

16. Owens, R. G., & Valesky, T. C. (2022). *Organizational behavior in education: Leadership and school reform* (12th ed.). Pearson Education.

17. Parfitt, C. M., Rea, D. C., Carter, C. F., Wilkerson, J. R., Rose, A. L., & Valesky, T. C. (2019). Assessing leadership dispositions: Does explicit instruction matter? *Southeast Journal of Educational Administration*, *19*(1), 67–77.

18. Jones, R. J., & Henry, M. (2019). Students' assessment of teacher quality: Recommendations for improvement. *Southeast Journal of Educational Administration*, *19*(1), 1–15.

19. McCall, M. W., Jr. (1997). *High flyers: Developing the next generation of leaders*. Harvard Business School Press.

20. Wilkerson, J. R., & Lang, W. S. (2007). *Assessing teacher dispositions: Five standards-based steps to valid measurement using the DAATS model*. Corwin Press.

21. *ibid.*

22. Chavez, J. (2011). The case for succession planning. *Strategic Finance*, *92*(8), 15–16.

23. Council of Chief State School Officers. (1996). *Interstate School Leaders Licensure Consortium standards for school leaders*. Author.

24. Council of Chief State School Officers. (2008). *Educational leadership policy standards*. Author.

25. Council of Chief State School Officers. (2008). *Performance expectations and indicators for educational leaders*. Author.

26. National Policy Board for Educational Administration. (2015). *Professional Standards for Educational Leaders*. Author.

27. *ibid.*—Rothwell (2005)

28. Conger, J. A., & Fulmer, R. M. (2003). Developing your leadership pipeline. *Harvard Business Review*, *81*(12), 76–84.

29. *ibid.*—Shaw, Erickson, & Harvey (2011)

30. *ibid.*—Parfitt (2017)

31. Thomas, J. G. (2011). *Exploring succession leadership training for continuity of leadership in selected K–12 school jurisdictions in Alberta* (Publication No. 3674163) [Doctoral dissertation, University of Phoenix]. ProQuest Dissertations and Theses Global.

32. Riddick, F. P. (2009). *What is your bench strength? An exploration of succession planning in three large school districts in a southeastern state* (Publication No. 3360378) [Doctoral dissertation, North Carolina State University]. ProQuest Dissertations and Theses Global.

33. *ibid.*—Steele (2015)

34. *ibid.*—Riddick (2009)

35. *ibid.*—Beeson (1998)

36. *ibid.*—Rothwell (2005)

37. Griffith, M. B. (2012). Effective succession planning in nursing: A review of the literature. *Journal of Nursing Management, 20*(7), 900–911. https://doi.org/10.1111/j.1365-2834.2012.01418.x

38. *ibid.*—Rothwell (2005)
39. *ibid.*—Beeson (1998)
40. Attributed to Gary Player, PGA Hall of Fame golf professional.
41. *ibid.*—Chavez (2011)

Chapter 3

Multiple Measures of Talent

Although the concept was addressed in the previous two chapters, the use of multiple measures of talent is a vital facet to succession planning and needs to be explored in greater depth. No matter how fair and objective one claims to be, there will always be some level of subjectivity in evaluations of personnel . . . simply a matter of human nature. Therefore, to ensure a quality succession-planning process, steps must be taken to mitigate biases. Using multiple raters is one prominent method to mitigate bias in identifying talent. But who needs to be involved?

ASK SIRI

Apple changed human interaction with personal technology in 2011 with the introduction of Siri with the iPhone, as an artificial intelligent personal assistant.[1] Asking Siri for a weather report for the following week or the website of a business is fine. However, asking Siri to identify talent is beyond the capability of the most sophisticated algorithms, as is asking who should be involved. Identifying the proper individual is the goal; although the most pressing question is this: "Who should one ask to be involved in talent identification?"

To answer the question effectively, one must review the best practices for decision-making processes. From his classic article in 1967, Edwin Bridges defined two tests for inclusion in the decision-making process: (a) the test of relevance and (b) the test of expertise.[2] In essence, if the individuals had relevance connected to outcome of the decision and had the expertise to contribute to the decision, then those who meet the requirements should be included. Robert Owens and Thomas Valesky added a third test—the test of jurisdiction.[3] Do the individuals have the jurisdictional authority to be involved in making the decision?

To explain the test of jurisdiction, an analogy would be that a professor of educational leadership has a child who attends an elementary school, and the principal needs to hire a new assistant principal. The decision affects the professor indirectly because of the enrolled child, and the professor clearly has expertise in educational leadership. So arguably, the professor meets Bridge's two requirements; however, the professor lacks the jurisdictional authority to be involved in the decision-making process. From a procedural standpoint, the individuals must meet all three of the tests to be considered in the decision-making process.

FREE FOR ALL?

Depending on the size and scope of the organization, should every possible individual who meets the three tests be involved? Such input would be beneficial, but most likely not feasible, nor would every single individual provide new information. Even though numerical scores may be used, the evaluation is essentially qualitative in nature. Using Catherine Marshall and Gretchen Rossman's research recommendation, the answer is to interview enough individuals to reach saturation,[4] or the point at which no new information is obtained.

However, caution must be used in compiling ordinal data.[5] If a person who analyzed results from a satisfaction survey designed with five-point Likert scale items provided means scores, he or she may have presented a false report. For example, a veteran assistant principal was transferred to a new school because of expertise with instructional leadership, and the soon-to-be-retiring principal recognized the need for increased student achievement and a review of long-standing procedures.

The new assistant principal instituted a revised format for lesson plans and held coaching conferences with every teacher to discuss strengths and weaknesses. However, a few teachers were very unhappy with the changes and refused to follow the requirements. After meeting with each teacher individually and explaining the requirements and expectations, the assistant principal gave a week for those teachers to comply. When they did not comply again, the assistant principal met with the principal and issued formal reprimands to those who refused to comply.

Those teachers became disgruntled and rated the assistant principal lowly on the survey. Only another handful of teachers completed the survey, all ranking the assistant principal highly favorable. Because of the small sample and inclusion of only diametric viewpoints, providing an average would yield a score approximately 3.0, seemingly average; yet, the raters ranked the assistant principal only as exceptional or dismal. An important question to understand is *why* was the individual rated as such?

Remember that subordinates are just as prone to influence of human emotions as supervisors. A former police chief once stated that just because someone has a complaint does not make the complaint valid.[6] Therefore, one must return to the question of why? Why did the reviewer *strongly agree* or *strongly disagree* on the assessment? What were the perceptions leading to the decision? Returning to the point of saturation, if seven reviewers all described a leadership candidate as micromanaging, would there be any need to ask another 10 or 20 or even 100 to receive the same feedback?

WHEN IS ENOUGH, ENOUGH?

Using the "gold standard" benchmark in evaluation—the Joint Committee for Educational Evaluation's *Program Evaluation Standards: A Guide for Evaluators and Evaluation Users* in which its authors stated that evaluations must not be conducted literally and superficially but rather adaptively to each unique situation[7]—every setting and review will be unique. Therefore, no universal answer exists.

Applying Marshall and Rossman's assertion to reach saturation[8] still does not provide an appropriate point from which to start because saturation is an end point. Then, considering the assertion that personnel evaluations are inherently qualitative in nature, using qualitative research processes is logical. An evaluation of talent meets Robert Stake's definition of a specific case bounded by time and space.[9] Furthermore, because reviews are collected from multiple individuals to provide a greater picture for one individual, the process could be defined using multiple case-study procedures,[10] and four to 10 is an appropriate starting point.[11]

There are potential negative aspects to consider; William Rothwell cautioned that multirater evaluations can be expensive for the organization and are only truly worthwhile if the individuals in senior leadership positions are clear about the vision and direction of the organization.[12] Furthermore, consideration must be given to the number of individuals evaluated and who is compiling the data. If a principal supervisor has 12 principals directly reporting to him or her, and every principal has 10 evaluations, then 120 individual evaluations must be compiled and analyzed.

ENOUGH TO COMPLETE THE CIRCLE

One important aspect to mention is that for an appropriate 360-degree assessment of talent, subordinates and superordinates two levels above and, if possible, below must be included. Also, peers, appropriate external stakeholders, and senior leaders if they are greater than two levels above the individual being assessed need to be included.[13] Prior to conducting any assessments, it is essential to have clearly defined specifications for the timeframe, to know who is collecting and analyzing the data, and to know how it will be used.[14] Transparency throughout the entire process is vital.[15]

WHAT IS TO BE ASSESSED?

Although who and roughly how many people are to be involved are important questions, a greater question remains. What specific aspects need to be evaluated? First, the feedback solicited must be targeted toward the purpose of identifying individuals with the knowledge, skills, and dispositions to be successful in the *future*. Quality succession planning is a process to ensure future organizational needs are met, although receiving appropriate feedback is "easier said than done."

The difference between talent appraisal and performance management was briefly discussed in Chapter 1.[16] The distinction is important because success at one level does not guarantee success in future positions. Talent appraisal is needed in an organization; regardless of identification of future potential, an individual must continue to demonstrate success in a current setting. So, current evaluations are one component of the process. However, the preeminent focus must be on the individual's *future suitability* for positions of greater authority.

Caution must be taken; far too often charisma is mistakenly used as a substitute for knowledge, skills, and dispositions, and when coupled with a focus on current job performance, erroneous results may be yielded.[17] Another common mistake is the reliance on stock instruments. At minimum, a previously created instrument must be revised to address the unique organizational culture, as well as criteria specific for the position to be assessed.[18]

Job, task, and position analyses are recommended approaches to determine the essential components to assess. In a job analysis, the activities, duties, functions, and responsibilities are defined. The specific steps to achieve each job component is the focus for a task analysis. A position analysis is unique to the role a specific individual has in the organization. For instance, a principal at Eastside Elementary School would have one defined position description, and the principal at Westside Elementary School would have another.

For those already in leadership positions, a component of the evaluation must also consider the extent to which he or she has ensured subordinates are prepared for positions of greater authority.[19] Michael Fullan framed the issue in terms of the school leader having an "exit plan" from the very first day.[20] Unfortunately, few school systems have metrics in place to rate how current leaders are preparing new leaders.

Although business or medical standards are not always directly applicable to an educational setting, there are valuable lessons. During his tenure as CEO of General Electric, Jack Welch placed a great emphasis on improvement. For mid-level managers and above, they were required to demonstrate how the lowest performing individuals made substantial improvements or were removed from their positions; otherwise, the manager was deemed ineffective and he or she was removed. Welch understood that hiring the proper individuals was the most important function of an executive.[21]

In fairness, Welch himself admitted to failing approximately 50% of the time early in his career but asserted he improved to 80% before retirement.[22] As mentioned previously, evaluations and assessments of personnel are part of a subjective process, and there is never a guarantee of success. The prominent management expert Peter Drucker once contended that most executives are only successful about one-third of the time in hiring decisions. Another third of hires are mediocre, and the final third are failures. Yet, managing personnel and staffing decisions should constitute the majority of an executive's time.[23]

BUILDING PROCESSES INTO THE CULTURE

While managing time appropriately for a school leader is vitally important—otherwise, he or she will spend an inordinate amount of time "putting out fires"[24]—but, an important facet is to establish sustainable aspects that remain beyond one's tenure in a leadership position.[25] Establishing a 360-degree assessment process or a multirater evaluation system for talent identification is a method to engage multiple stakeholders and ensure processes remain beyond one's time in a position.

CONCLUDING THOUGHTS

Based on the concepts discussed in this chapter, Figure 3.1 contains a checklist to determine the extent to which multiple measures are used to identify

Multiple Measures Checklist

1. What is my role in the organization?
   - [ ] Superintendent
   - [ ] Assistant Superintendent/Principal Supervisor
   - [ ] Principal
   - [ ] Assistant Principal
   - [ ] Other Administrator
   - [ ] Curriculum Specialist/Instructional Coach
   - [ ] Grade Level or Subject Chair
   - [ ] Classroom Teacher
   - [ ] Support Staff
   - [ ] Parent or Student
   - [ ] External

2. Does the organization have established requirements or a succession plan already? If so, be sure to follow institutional processes.

3. Based on my role, do I have jurisdictional authority to hire a person for the next lower level?

4. How many levels are above me in the organization (superordinates)?

5. How many levels are below me in the organization (subordinates)?

6. Based on the answers to questions 1 through 5, tentatively determine who should be involved? Individuals without jurisdictional authority should encourage superordinates to be involved in the process actively.

7. Are there defined job, task, and position descriptions?

8. Is an evaluation system that considers the specific and unique organizational culture in place?

9. Is ensuring preparation of future leaders a component of the evaluation?

10. Is the evaluation designed to determine future suitability for a leadership position, not just determine current job success or charisma?

11. Based on question 7 through 10, creation or revision of assessment criteria and instruments are needed.

12. After an official instrument is ready, have a timeframe, purpose, and procedures for collecting and analyzing data been established and conveyed?

Figure 3.1. Multiple Measures of Talent Checklist

leadership talent. Because the organizational culture is very different in every organization, as is the structure, the first questions are designed to help establish positionality in the organizational hierarchy. Then based on role, questions to determine if the processes in place are included.

For example, in a very small school district, there may only be three levels in a school setting: teachers and non-instructional staff members, a few principals, and a superintendent. Whereas a very large school district may employ instructional coaches or quasi-administrators before assistant principals, and between the principal and superintendent it may have multiple levels of directors or assistant/associate/deputy superintendents. One does not need to be a chief executive to ensure individuals are prepared to assume positions of greater authority, and individuals must be prepared at every level of the organization.

Although the use of multiple measures is primarily a concern for determining suitability of internal candidates to be promoted, all of the appropriate stakeholders should be part of interview committees to examine external candidates. Judging the suitability of promoting an internal candidate compared to hiring an external candidate is the focus of the next chapter. Regardless of the focus, the process needs to be open and transparent at every level because the ultimate goal is to have qualified individuals at every level ready to assume greater responsibility.

CHAPTER REFERENCES

1. Dormehl, L. (2020, October 4). *Today in Apple history: Siri debuts on iPhone 4s*. Cult of Mac. https://www.cultofmac.com/447783/today-in-apple-history-siri-makes-its-public-debut-on-iphone-4s/

2. Bridges, E. M. (1967). A model for shared decision making in the school principalship. *Educational Administration Quarterly, 3*(1), 52–59.

3. Owens, R. G., & Valesky, T. C. (2022). *Organizational behavior in education: Leadership and school reform* (12th ed.). Pearson Education.

4. Marshall, C., & Rossman, G. B. (1999). *Designing qualitative research* (3rd ed.). Sage Publications.

5. Kuzon, W., Urbanchek, M., & McCabe, S. (1996). The seven deadly sins of statistical analysis. *Annals of Plastic Surgery, 37*, 265–272.

6. Attributed to Richard A. Parfitt, M.A., C.T.M., P.S.P., former chief of police, Florida Southwestern State College.

7. Yarbrough, D. B., Shulha, L. M., Hopson, R. K., & Caruthers, F. A. (2011). *The program evaluation standards: A guide for evaluators and evaluation users* (3rd ed.). Sage Publications.

8. *ibid.*—Marshall & Rossman (1999)

9. Stake, R. E. (1995). *The art of case study research*. Sage Publications.

10. *ibid.*

11. Gentles, S. J., Charles, C., Ploeg, J., & McKibbon, K. (2015). Sampling in qualitative research: Insights from an overview of the methods literature. *Qualitative Report*, *20*(11), 1772–1789. https://nsuworks.nova.edu/tqr/vol20/iss11/5/

12. Rothwell, W. J. (2005). *Effective succession planning: Ensuring leadership continuity and building talent from within* (3rd ed.). AMACOM.

13. Beeson, J. (1998). Succession planning: Building the management corps. *Business Horizons*, *41*(5), 61–66.

14. *ibid.*—Rothwell (2005).

15. Meyer, M. J., Macmillan, R. B., & Northfield, S. (2009). Principal succession and its impact on teacher morale. *International Journal of Leadership in Education: Theory and Practice*, *12*(2), 171–185. https://doi.org/10.1080/13603120802449660

16. *ibid.*—Rothwell (2005)

17. Chavez, J. (2011). The case for succession planning. *Strategic Finance*, *92*(8), 15–16.

18. *ibid.*—Rothwell (2005)

19. Smeltzer, C. H. (2002). Succession planning. *Journal of Nursing Administration*, *32*(12), 615.

20. Fullan, M. (2005). *Sustainable leadership.* Corwin Press.

21. Fernández-Aráoz, C. (2020, March 3). Jack Welch's approach to leadership. *Harvard Business Review*. https://hbr.org/2020/03/jack-welchs-approach-to-leadership

22. *ibid.*

23. Drucker, P. F. (1985, July). How to make people decisions. *Harvard Business Review*. https://hbr.org/1985/07/how-to-make-people-decisions

24. *ibid.*—Owens & Valesky (2022)

25. Hargreaves, A., & Fink, D. (2006). *Sustainable leadership.* Jossey-Bass.

Chapter 4

Internal versus External Sources of Talent

Sage advice to determine the need to hire an external individual for a high-level position is directly connected to the departure of the most recent person. If there were scandals or deep-seated and negative cultural aspects, then an outsider should be hired. Unfortunately, deeply entrenched cultural components may take a generation to change.[1] Absent major scandals, are there other times to consider an external individual over internal candidates?

NO WAXING PLATITUDES

One of the most important concepts addressed throughout each chapter is the importance of honoring the unique organizational culture. Therefore, every positional vacancy must be viewed as a unique opportunity, and a simple formula will not suffice. Ultimately, professional judgment needs to occur. The debate between internal and external candidates was briefly addressed in Chapter 2, and the true question to be addressed is the determination of future potential as evidenced by the knowledge, skills, and dispositions.

William Rothwell,[2] along with Jay Conger and Robert Fulmer,[3] were cited previously, and their assertions were quite clear to establish a pipeline of quality internal candidates. Understanding the unique organizational culture is one of the prime benefits to choosing an internal candidate. However, the "downside" to choosing an internal candidate will be the fact he or she will have preconceived biases from immersion in the culture. So, the need for organizational change will impact the decision.

ALL THINGS BEING EQUAL

Considering a well-functioning organization with a positive culture and two candidates with approximately equal credentials—one internal and one external—then the preference would be to promote the internal candidate. Mainly because there will be a "learning curve" for an external candidate, who must handle responsibilities while learning the culture. Using Linda Lee's three considerations for succession, the logical choice would be a planned-continuity approach.[4] The internal candidate would be given the task of continuing to move the organization forward in the same direction.

However, planned discontinuity does not require an external candidate. As Linda Lee indicated, planned discontinuity still would require the incoming individual to have an appropriate transition and an understanding of the unique organizational culture. The major difference is that the new leader is expected to make changes for organizational improvement. One important consideration is John Beeson's assertion that talent be viewed as an organization-wide asset.[5] Just because an individual is serving as an assistant principal in one school should not preclude him or her from eventually serving as principal in a different setting, nor require it.

Having an organization-wide pool of talent will be needed to have a quality succession-planning process. A number of business authors[6] and nursing authors[7] clearly recommended having robust internal processes to promote from within the organization. Although professional development and mentoring will be covered in chapters 6 through 9, the importance must be mentioned now. Identified individuals need to have appropriate "stretch" assignments[8] to provide opportunities for them to develop skills beyond those needed for a current position.

Regardless of the position, the appropriate 360-degree assessments must be conducted. Any aspects for the next greater level with which the individual does not have experience should be noted in the assessment and included in the development plan for the next year.[9] The next-level supervisor must then be evaluated on preparing subordinates for greater positions of authority, just as the current individual is responsible for preparing future successors. Mary Griffith, a nursing succession-planning researcher, contended that supervisors have a moral imperative to prepare others to assume positions of greater authority.[10]

Whether considering an internal candidate or bringing an external person into the organization, the determination has to be on the suitability for success *in the future*. The determination should be forward thinking to consider future positions, not just the next promotion.[11] In essence, a person should not be hired to be a "good" assistant principal; he or she should have the knowledge, skills, and dispositions to be a successful principal and beyond.

BENEFITING FROM MULTIPLE VIEWPOINTS

In addition to identifying talent, utilizing multiple viewpoints in assessment can also help identify aspects in the subcultures. Every entity within the organization has multiple subcultures.[12] An astute executive leader can use the information to address the subcultures—whether to perpetuate positive aspects or, through planned discontinuity, to change negative ones. Care must be taken to evaluate the information objectively, however.

Multiple measures of talent was the focus of the prior chapter, so the information need not be reiterated. However, one should note that a 360-degree assessment can provide important information on the current readiness for an internal candidate. If an organization's senior leaders have yet to adopt robust succession-planning processes, then hiring an external candidate may be necessary. However, as Lou Sabina and Chris Colwell noted, hiring external candidates provides a unique set of challenges.[13]

In addition to the assessment of internal candidates, multiple viewpoints should be included on interview committees. Each group of stakeholders will presumably have a different focus. Teachers, support-staff members, students, principals of other schools, and principal supervisors will view candidates to be an assistant principal differently, and all of those viewpoints should be included.

CLEANING UP SOMEONE ELSE'S MESS

Far too often, an individual is promoted or transferred into a position just to address some real or perceived inadequacy in the organization. Minimal to no thought is given to the organizational culture or how changes will be received. Without support or buy-in from the current teachers and staff, new initiatives are often unsuccessful. Because teachers typically remain in the same position longer than principals, many experienced teachers will resist unfavorable changes and wait for the next administrative change.[14]

Therein lies another problem—the rapid, but intentional turnover of principals. The concept of a turnaround principal is not new, just as the desire to find a panacea in education. The primary issue with the typical model is the expectation for an individual to achieve success rapidly and then be moved to another setting to repeat the feat. There is rarely consideration for the cultures of the different schools, and rapid turnover is antithetical to best practices.

Andy Hargreaves contended that a principal should be left in a position for five or more years.[15] Additionally, there is sufficient evidence to show that a change of principal in four or fewer years results in lower student achievement.[16] Because the impact of a principal is greatly affected by a predecessor, Hargreaves asserted that the most effective strategy to establish continuity is to limit the number and frequency of transfers.[17]

Although experienced teachers may attempt to resist changes and wait for a new principal to be appointed, instability in the position as principal has a detrimental effect on retention of younger teachers.[18] Newer teachers had a greater likelihood of seeking employment elsewhere if a change of principal is made within three or fewer years.[19] Leadership instability is detrimental for the school culture and climate.

Returning to the point that a turnaround expert is often needed for a lower performing school, he or she should remain in the position for several years to ensure the changes become part of the culture. Brianne Lopez-Romano documented facets of successful turnaround principals in Florida through a qualitative study. She found that successful turnaround principals were very conscious of the culture, openly communicated expectations, were very tenacious in meeting goals, used data-informed processes, and had a preeminent focus on instructional leadership.[20]

RIDING ON ANOTHER'S COATTAILS

However, just because a person assisted in some capacity in a successful organization does not guarantee continued success. An assistant principal who focused on testing schedules, discipline management, and lunch duty at a successful school is not necessarily prepared to be principal at the same school. Again, highlighting William Rothwell's focus on performance management, not simply assessment of success in a current position.[21]

Too often, time in a position is used as a determining factor for promoting an individual. Longevity and fidelity to an organization can be positive factors but should not be mistaken for knowledge, skills, and dispositions. John Beeson warned against using loyalty and a sense of personal trust as metrics for talent identification.[22] Hence, use of 360-degree assessments to identify new leaders is recommended.

PITFALLS FOR INTERNAL CANDIDATES

As mentioned at the beginning of the chapter, entrenched, negative aspects in the culture would be a reason to hire an external candidate. One of the dangers of ineffective internal promotion is the perpetuation of destructive leadership practices.[23] Of particular concern is the fact that many are unaware of the true nature of the practices. For example, an assistant principal who spent seven years working with a supervisor who minimized and tried to hide safety issues will most likely unconsciously learn to do the same.

Another concern for promoting an internal candidate is the possibility of an individual supervising former colleagues. Although there is a lack of scholarly material pertaining to supervision of former colleagues, there are plenty of trade articles and columns in which the author provides advice for transitioning from peer to supervisor.[24] Depending on the nature of the promotion and the duration with which an individual served as a colleague, the challenges can be vastly different.

BENEFITS FOR INTERNAL CANDIDATES

Although there are several "pitfalls" for promoting an internal candidate, there are equally as many benefits. Nursing researchers Sylvain Trepanier and Jeannette Crenshaw discussed equal benefits and risks associated with choosing an internal compared to an external candidate; however, one of the key benefits for choosing an internal candidate is the level of control for providing development opportunities.[25] Targeted and specific development and mentoring are the second major phase in quality succession planning and will be discussed in greater depth in chapters 8 and 9.

Perpetuation of destructive leadership practices is a concern for promoting internal candidates; however, perpetuation of a healthy, positive organizational culture is a benefit. Having a thorough understanding of the organizational nuances is a positive aspect and will help a new leader "navigate the waters." Michael Fullan asserted that a new leader must focus on sustainability from the very first day in the position.[26] Sustainability is achieved through the usage of distributed leadership.[27]

NEGATIVES FOR EXTERNAL CANDIDATES

There are plenty of reasons why business experts recommend promoting internally. There are also many challenges, and the same is true for external candidates. Lou Sabina and Chris Colwell addressed several of the challenges in hiring an external candidate, including resentment from internal candidates who were not promoted, lack of support from senior leaders, and unfamiliarity with the organizational culture and climate.[28]

While the lack of understanding of the organizational culture is a substantial challenge for an external candidate, another important facet for senior leaders to understand is that equivalent titles and positions do not equal equivalent experience. A superintendent for a small midwestern town with a total population of 300 students will have a drastically different experience than one who served as superintendent for a large county-based metropolitan district. Some of the most noticeable differences involve those who serve as assistant principals. One may be the de facto senior administrator, while another only has limited responsibilities.[29]

POSITIVES FOR EXTERNAL CANDIDATES

The prime reason for selecting an external candidate was already listed; to address a negative organizational culture or recovery from scandal or other issues. However, a less extreme reason is to have an external person bring new ideas to the organization.[30] Additionally, an external person may be hired because of a unique or special skill set that no current internal candidate possesses.

Additionally, having a person's first experience in an organization be in a leadership role can allow for a "fresh start." Stakeholders are not viewed with preconceived notions from an external candidate. An external person can bring new partnerships to a school or district. Furthermore, an external person is not beholden to the precedents of those who came before to the same degree an internal person will be.[31] Regardless of the prior employment status, a person must be the proper fit for the organizational culture. Period.

CONCLUDING THOUGHTS

While practical suggestions were given pertaining to reasons for selecting internal or external candidates for leadership positions, those decisions must always be secondary to the questions of proper fit with the organizational culture. As a general rule, the circumstances of the departure of the previous individual should be considered. Then, using Linda Lee's options for planned continuity or planned discontinuity, decisions must be made on the continued direction for the organization.

In building upon the concepts of the previous chapters, the use of multiple measures for assessing internal candidates, or hiring committees to choose an external candidate, are needed. Different groups of stakeholders will have varying perspectives, and each must be considered. Finally, the true assessment must be based on potential success in the future, and not solely based

Internal Versus External Scorecard

Directions. Mark the internal or external column based on the situation. Compile the totals at the bottom.

Question	Internal	External
1. If the current organizational culture/climate is positive and does not need to be changed, mark internal.		
2. If there have been compliance issues or other management problems, mark external.		
3. If having "inside" knowledge will be beneficial for the individual, mark internal.		
4. Are there sufficient individuals with preferred qualifications to be successful, if so, mark internal.		
5. Unless several current employees are ready to assume the position immediately, mark external.		
6. Do most groups of stakeholders view the organization as successful currently? If not, mark external.		
7. Based on external metrics (e.g., state assessment grade), is the organization functioning successfully? If not, mark external.		
8. Does a robust professional development or training program current exist? If so, mark internal.		
9. Is there sufficient time for a new leader to become enculturated in the position. If no, mark internal.		
10. Have prior individuals who have been promoted internally been successful? If not, mark external.		

Total Number of Internal _____
Total Number of External _____

Figure 4.1. Internal versus External Scorecard

on current success in a position. See Figure 4.1 for some general questions to assist in knowing if the circumstances favor an internal or external candidate.

CHAPTER REFERENCES

1. Attributed to Richard A. Parfitt, M.A., C.T.M., P.S.P., former chief of police, Florida Southwestern State College.
2. Rothwell, W. J. (2005). *Effective succession planning: Ensuring leadership continuity and building talent from within* (3rd ed.). AMACOM.
3. Conger, J. A., & Fulmer, R. M. (2003). Developing your leadership pipeline. *Harvard Business Review*, *81*(12), 76–84.
4. Lee, L. C. (2015). School performance trajectories and the challenges for principal succession. *Journal of Educational Administration*, *53*(2), 262–286. https://doi.org/10.1108/JEA-12-2012-0139
5. Beeson, J. (1998). Succession planning: Building the management corps. *Business Horizons*, *41*(5), 61–66.
6. e.g., *ibid.*—Beeson (1998)
ibid.—Conger & Fulmer (2003)
ibid.—Rothwell (2005)
7. e.g., Beglinger, J. E. (2013). Designing tomorrow: Creative and effective succession planning. *Journal of Nursing Administration*, *43*(10), 495–496. https://doi.org/10.1097/NNA.0b013e3182a3e85b
Griffith, M. B. (2012). Effective succession planning in nursing: A review of the literature. *Journal of Nursing Management*, *20*(7), 900–911. https://doi.org/10.1111/j.1365-2834.2012.01418.x
8. Chavez, J. (2011). The case for succession planning. *Strategic Finance*, *92*(8), 15–16.
9. Brittingham S. L. (2009). Principal succession in a fast-growing district. *School Administrator*, *66*(11), 22–25. https://aasa.org/SchoolAdministratorArticle.aspx?id=10144
10. Smeltzer, C. H. (2002). Succession planning. *Journal of Nursing Administration*, *32*(12), 615.
11. *ibid.*—Rothwell (2005)
12. Owens, R. G., & Valesky, T. C. (2022). *Organizational behavior in education: Leadership and school reform* (12th ed.). Pearson Education.
13. Sabina, L. L., & Colwell, C. (2018). Challenges of principal succession: Examining the challenges of hiring internal vs. external candidates. *Athens Journal of Education*, *5*(4), 375–396.
14. Snyder, R. R. (2017). Resistance to change among veteran teachers: Providing voice for more effective engagement. *International Journal of Educational Leadership Preparation*, *12*(1), 19–32. https://www.icpel.org/uploads/1/5/6/2/15622000/ijelp_volume_12_number_1__spring_2017_.pdf
15. Hargreaves, A. (2005). Leadership succession. *Educational Forum*, *69*(2), 163–173. https://doi.org/10.1080/00131720508984680

16. Zepeda, S. J., Bengtson, E., & Parylo, O. (2012). Examining the planning and management of principal succession. *Journal of Educational Administration, 50*(2), 136–158. https://doi.org/10.1108/09578231211210512

17. *ibid.*—Hargreaves (2005)

18. Meyer, M. J., Macmillan, R. B., & Northfield, S. (2009). Principal succession and its impact on teacher morale. *International Journal of Leadership in Education: Theory and Practice, 12*(2), 171–185. https://doi.org/10.1080/13603120802449660

19. Steele, F. G. (2015). *Principal experiences of succession planning* (Publication No. 10012699) [Doctoral dissertation, Oklahoma State University]. ProQuest Dissertations and Theses Global.

20. Lopez-Romano, B. M. (2021). *Turnaround principals' practices in the southeastern United States: A case study* (Publication No. 28412619) [Doctoral dissertation, University of West Florida]. ProQuest Dissertations and Theses Global.

21. *ibid.*—Rothwell (2005)

22. *ibid.*—Beeson (1998)

23. Shaw, J. B., Erickson, A., & Harvey, M. (2011). A method for measuring destructive leadership and identifying types of destructive leaders in organizations. *Leadership Quarterly, 22*(4), 575–590. https://doi.org/10.1016/j.leaqua.2011.05.001

24. i.e., Quast, L. (2013, September 30). 8 tips to transition from co-worker to manager. *Forbes.* https://www.forbes.com/sites/lisaquast/2013/09/30/8-tips-to-transition-from-co-worker-to-manager/?sh=4a4465c814b5

25. Trepanier, S., & Crenshaw, J. T. (2013). Succession planning: A call to action for nurse executives. *Journal of Nursing Management, 21*(7), 980–985. https://doi.org/10.111/jonm.12177

26. Fullan, M. (2005). *Sustainable leadership.* Corwin Press.

27. Hargreaves, A., & Fink, D. (2006). *Sustainable leadership.* Jossey-Bass.

28. *ibid.*—Sabina & Colwell (2018)

29. Hausman, C., Nebeker, A., McCreary, J., & Donaldson, G. (2002). The worklife of the assistant principal. *Journal of Educational Administration, 40*(2/3), 136–157. https://doi.org/10.1108/09578230210421105

30. *ibid.*—Sabina & Colwell (2018)

31. *ibid.*

Chapter 5

Characteristics of High-Potential Talent

The foci of the preceding chapters have been on varying aspects of talent identification. Before concluding this set of chapters, a brief discussion of the characteristics for success is needed, One important point is that there are no universal characteristics for all great leaders. A person may be the perfect individual for a particular setting and at a certain time, and then completely fail in another, even similar situation.[1]

For any position in an educational organization, an individual must have the proper knowledge, skills, and dispositions.[2] Knowledge and skills are somewhat more straightforward than dispositions, but all three are equally important. Of those three, assessment of dispositions is frequently omitted and is the component with which the least number of people are familiar. Although dispositions can be assessed through a morality lens, the most appropriate approach for leadership assessment is the extent to which a candidate's dispositions align to specific job-related standards.[3]

Case Study 5.1 contains information and a setting for fictional applicants for an assistant principal vacancy. The strengths and weaknesses of each candidate will be discussed throughout the chapter. The goal for the reader is to make a proper assessment with the information given as to which candidate should be recommended to become the next assistant principal at fictional Garner Elementary School.

ATTITUDES, VALUES, AND BELIEFS

Among the five candidates for the assistant principal position, understanding their dispositions will be very important. What attitudes, values, and beliefs would they bring to the position, and how do those dispositions align with the organizational culture and goals? Because each of the candidates will bring

Case Study 5.1

Finding a New Right Hand

You have been serving as principal of Garner Elementary School, a kindergarten through fifth-grade building with approximately 900 students in a predominantly suburban area for the past four years. The school has 45 regular classrooms—seven per grade level—along with full-time cocurricular teachers for general music, band and orchestra, visual arts, physical education, technology, plus curriculum specialists for math, language arts, and science, along with two certified counselors and two special education teachers. There are also 10 support staff members who handle the various office, custodial and records requirements.

Last Friday, the superintendent notified you that Mr. Thomas Chang, the assistant principal was being promoted to principal of the neighboring Erroll Elementary School. Mr. Chang had been assistant principal for six years and was hired by your predecessor. He had a good rapport with the teachers, staff members, students, and families. Some teachers have subtly expressed a desire to follow Mr. Chang to Erroll Elementary School.

While student performance as rated by the state-mandated assessments has been improving every year since your appointment as principal, the growth is not sufficient to meet the district strategic goals. Although there was some turnover among the teachers for the first year after being appointed principal, 39 teachers have been employed at the school for five or more years, with 17 being employed 20 or more years at the school. There are clearly two distinct groups of teachers: a younger group and a veteran group.

Based on school-district policy, human-resources representatives review all applicants for administrative positions and determine eligibility, then only the qualified names are forwarded to the hiring manager for consideration. Although three teachers at Garner Elementary School have appropriate state certification to serve as an assistant principal, one teacher had only three years of instructional experience and was deemed ineligible; she is quite displeased with the school district and with you because of the determination.

Although you have hired instructional support teachers and assisted with screening interviews for entry into the administrative pool, this vacancy is the first opportunity for you to hire an administrator. The following list of applicants are to be considered. Throughout the chapter, additional information will be provided for each candidate.

Brian Rivera has 12 years' teaching experience in various elementary grades, all in Northside Elementary School, which is geographically at the opposite side of the region in a neighboring district. The school is smaller, and the student population is vastly different with substantially lower achievement scores. The culture at Northside is not known to be very collaborative. Mr. Rivera does not have documented experience in supervising teachers other than his master's-degree internship.

Melissa Lee has 7 years' teaching experience at your school; however, she did not become a teacher until she was in her 30s. Ms. Lee is enrolled in a doctoral program at a major state university and is well respected by peers. She has aspirations to be employed in higher education. Ms. Lee just became the kindergarten chair last school year; although she has presented at leadership conferences with several of her professors, she has no other practical leadership experience.

Amanda Flowers has 6 years' teaching experience in the school district. For the past two years, she has been the curriculum specialist for Veterans Elementary School. Ms. Flowers is very dependable and always willing to accept new responsibilities. She was a highly effective teacher and has a grasp of standards and pedagogy. Although she has experience evaluating teachers, her current principal has indicated that she can be very self-conscious with the fact she has to assist teachers who are more than double her age.

David Miller has 27 years' teaching experience at your school. He knows the community and the families well. Having been passed over for the position as assistant principal twice before, Mr. Miller does not have a positive view of the district process and has indicated that if he does not receive the promotion that he will leave the school. Despite serving at the same school for years, Mr. Miller has never sought opportunities for leadership development.

Wendy McPatrick has 21 years' teaching experience in a neighboring district. She was teacher of the year a few years ago. Ms. McPatrick has experience in schools vastly different from Garner Elementary School, as most were located in very affluent neighborhoods. Her recommendations and application materials are impeccable. Of note, she has been employed at nine different schools over the 21 years.

Figure 5.1. Finding a New Right Hand

slightly different dispositions to the position, a mismatch of dispositions to organizational culture can be a "recipe for disaster."

Because of the fact only outward signs of the internalized attitudes, values, and beliefs are shown, assessments must be self-reported or have a reliance on another's interpretation of outward behavior. For the greatest accuracy, multiple measures of dispositions are needed.[4] Fortunately, there is a positive correlation between exposure to standards-based dispositions through leadership coursework and self-reported beliefs aligned to standards.[5] Furthermore, in his doctoral dissertation, Kyle LaPaglia has shown that undergraduate students' dispositions improved throughout an education preparation program.[6]

GENERAL TRAITS

Some authors have argued that perpetuation of values is of greater importance in succession planning than knowledge or skills.[7] So, are there general characteristics that are beneficial for leadership candidates to have? Most certainly. Effective leaders are usually authentic, trustworthy, caring, passionate, and value driven. They are willing to take appropriate risks while admitting failure, are open minded, and have an ability to listen to others empathetically.[8] Effective leaders are also open to feedback from all stakeholders.[9]

Identifying characteristics are helpful, but all too often, the focus of succession planning is simply ensuring one replacement is prepared, rather than a robust process for developing the skill set for a pool of qualified potential successors.[10] However, care must be taken not to seek "clones" of the current leader. John Beeson discussed the importance of skill development and flexibility because a rapidly changing business environment meant positions of today might not exist tomorrow.[11]

Use of distributed leadership was defined as a tool for flexibility and to perpetuate positive cultural aspects and mitigate issues that arise from administrative transition.[12] Furthermore, the use of distributed leadership fosters open communication and trust among teachers and staff members. To be effective, leaders must not simply espouse a desire to implement distributed leadership, they must actively ensure distributed leadership is a thoroughly integrated component of the culture. By addressing the culture and giving voice to stakeholders, morale is often increased as well.[13]

Returning to the five applicants, indication of dispositions may be given in interview responses, but evidence should also be considered from materials from supervisors and colleagues. As Judy Wilkerson and Steve Lang indicated, multiple measures of dispositions are needed. Therefore, in addition to the information provided in Figure 5.1, some key phrases from recommendation letters will help identify the proper individual to become the next assistant principal.

Mr. Rivera had a letter from a renowned professor who stated that he was among the top 10% of all students and had great potential to lead effectively. Having directly observed Ms. Lee for four years, she attends every extracurricular event, and often is in the building for 10 hours every day. Ms. Flowers has glowing recommendations, and a notable line was "in a time when common sense is no longer common, Amanda has an abundance." Mr. Miller is seen as a de facto spokesman for veteran teachers. The recommendation for Ms. McPatrick from a former principal said that she "excels with curricular aspects."

PROPER EXPERIENCE

To be effective, the required experience and skills must be listed appropriately in the job description and advertisement material for the position, and be conveyed effectively to all potential applicants, as well as the internal stakeholders.[14] From an organization-wide perspective, there must be consistency. For example, if five years' teaching experience is a requirement to be promoted to assistant principal, do not consider any internal *or* external candidates who do not meet the minimum requirements.

Promoting unqualified candidates for political reasons creates negative aspects in the culture and is detrimental to trust and communication.[15] There are also many other subtle issues that are evident in organizations with a negative culture. Common themes among organizations with a negative culture may include increased absenteeism, increased "presenteeism" (i.e., working while ill), as well as lower levels of performance and productivity plus a greater desire for individuals to seek employment elsewhere.[16] Among the worst possibilities are potential for litigation because a person perceived discriminatory treatment—regardless of truth.[17]

Conversely, actively engaging all relevant stakeholders in an open and transparent process increases trust and engagement, and by doing so there is a greater likelihood that teachers will focus on long-term needs and goals because they are active participants in the organizational direction.[18] Having the proper experience is not a guarantee of success;[19] however, ensuring the person selected meets—or preferably exceeds—all of the minimum qualifications will greatly help the person make the necessary transition.

IS THE EXPERIENCE COMMENSURATE?

A very important fact is that not all experience is commensurate or equal, and the context must be considered. An individual who spent 10 years as a teacher at a small, exclusive, suburban private school presumably will not be well prepared to serve in a position of greater authority at a rural or urban school unless he or she had other experiences, and vice versa. Depending on the setting and context, an individual who has spent an entire professional career in an elementary school is probably not the best candidate to be promoted to a high school assistant principal position.

Consideration of all of an individual's characteristics matters, and it must be made within the view of the unique organizational culture.[20] Yes, Morgan McCall defined appropriate experience as one of the components to having the "right stuff."[21] Providing the appropriate experiences will be discussed in greater detail in the following chapters. Often, discretion must be given to which experiences are needed most. An important reiteration is that consideration is not just for the present but also for the future.[22]

Considering the job posting for the fictional position contained a specification for a minimum of five years classroom experience (district requirement), preferably at the elementary level, and with two years in a quasi-leadership role (department chair, curriculum specialist, etc . . .), then the leadership experience potentially can be a differentiator immediately. Mr. Rivera, Mr. Miller, and Ms. McPatrick do not have experience outside of a regular classroom. Presuming the current school year is over half concluded, Ms. Lee has just under two year's leadership experience and Ms. Flowers has about the same but in a coaching position.

REQUISITE EDUCATION

Just as proper experience is needed, appropriate educational credentials are also required. All 50 states have certification requirements for educational leadership—usually at the master's or specialist level.[23] Because of the state requirements, every person considered for the position must have the appropriate educational credentials. However, not all leadership preparation programs are equal, and the level of preparation is an important component.[24] Although for appropriate succession planning collaborative partnerships between school districts and institutions of higher education should be established.[25]

For individuals identified for future development, funding to offset the costs of higher education should be budgeted annually.[26] Collaborative partnerships can be mutually beneficial for all parties and are also options that have positive correlations for student achievement.[27] Just be sure multiple measures are used for identification of talent and the individuals have the knowledge, skills, and dispositions for success now and in the future.

CONCLUDING THOUGHTS

While there are no truly universal characteristics of all great leaders, there are general characteristics found in many. Matching a person's knowledge, skills, and dispositions to the position and requirement is important, but an alignment of values to the organizational culture is imperative. He or she must have the proper education and commensurate experience, which in turn provide credibility for the individual. The old saying, "been there; done that" matters, because people can always tell when someone has not.

Returning one last time to the fictional applicants, which one has the knowledge, skills, dispositions, education, experience, and credibility to be the next assistant principal at Garner Elementary School? The choices were designed to narrow the applicants considerably. In reality, there probably is no perfect candidate, so decisions will need to be made pertaining to the suitability for *future* success.

Even for a fictional account, enough information cannot be provided to address all of the aspects; though, hopefully the reader would have narrowed the choice to Ms. Flowers and Ms. Lee. Mr. Rivera, Mr. Miller, and Ms. McPatrick have positive qualities but lack several of the needed experiences and, in some cases, dispositions. To provide closure, a brief assessment of each candidate is provided.

Mr. Rivera has potential but, with the information provided, lacks the quasi-administrative experience, and the school setting is not necessarily commensurate with Garner Elementary School. Ms. Lee has experience in the setting and has potential, but she also has some weaknesses. If current understanding of the culture matters more than supervisory experience, she is probably the best choice. Ms. Flowers has the closest experience needed, but is consideration in working with veteran teachers needed? Mr. Miller has experience at the school but also the potential to be a negative influence. Finally, Ms. McPatrick has plenty of experience but not stability.

CHAPTER REFERENCES

1. McCall, M. W., Jr. (1997). *High flyers: Developing the next generation of leaders*. Harvard Business School Press.
2. Wilkerson, J. R., & Lang, W. S. (2007). *Assessing teacher dispositions: Five standards-based steps to valid measurement using the DAATS model*. Corwin Press.

3. Wilkerson, J. R. (2006, April 20). Measuring teacher dispositions: Standards-based or morality-based? *Teachers College Record*, ID Number 12493. http://www.tcrecord.org/Content.asp?ContentID=12493

4. *ibid.*—Wilkerson & Lang (2007)

5. Parfitt, C. M., Rea, D. C., Carter, C. F., Wilkerson, J. R., Rose, A. L., & Valesky, T. C. (2019). Assessing leadership dispositions: Does explicit instruction matter? *Southeast Journal of Educational Administration*, *19*(1), 67–77.

6. LaPaglia, K. (2020). *Preservice teacher dispositions: A case study of changes during a teacher preparation program* (Publication No. 28314521) [Doctoral dissertation, Florida Gulf Coast University]. ProQuest Dissertations and Theses Global.

7. Beglinger, J. E. (2014). Designing tomorrow: Changing our practice in response to evidence. *Journal of Nursing Administration*, *44*(4), 194–195. https://doi.org/10.1097/NNA.0000000000000055

8. Chavez, J. (2011). The case for succession planning. *Strategic Finance*, *92*(8), 15–16.

9. Beeson, J. (1998). Succession planning: Building the management corps. *Business Horizons*, *41*(5), 61–66.

10. Mehribani, S. E., & Mohammed, N. A. (2011). Succession planning: A necessary process in today's organization. *International Journal of e-Education, e-Business, e-Management, and e-Learning*, *1*(5), 371–377.

11. Beeson, J. (2000). Succession planning: Leading-edge practices: What the best companies are doing. *Across the Board*, *37*(2), 38–41.

12. Hargreaves, A. (2005). Leadership succession. *Educational Forum*, *69*(2), 163–173. https://doi.org/10.1080/00131720508984680

13. Meyer, M. J., Macmillan, R. B., & Northfield, S. (2009). Principal succession and its impact on teacher morale. *International Journal of Leadership in Education: Theory and Practice*, *12*(2), 171–185. https://doi.org/10.1080/13603120802449660

14. Rothwell, W. J. (2005). *Effective succession planning: Ensuring leadership continuity and building talent from within* (3rd ed.). AMACOM.

15. Macmillan, R. B., Meyer, M. J., & Northfield, S. (2014). Trust and its role in principal succession: A preliminary examination of a continuum of trust. *Leadership and Policy in Schools*, *3*(4), 275–294. https://doi.org/10.1080/15700760490901993

16. Cowan, R. L. (2018). When workplace bullying and mobbing occur: The impact on organizations. In M. Duffy & D. C. Yamada (Eds.), *Workplace bullying and mobbing in the United States* (Volume 1, pp. 201–218). Praeger.

17. Erden, P., & Otken, A. B. (2019). The dark side of paternalistic leadership: Employee discrimination and nepotism. *European Research Studies Journal*, *22*(2), 154–180.

18. *ibid.*—Meyer, Macmillan, & Northfield (2009)

19. *ibid.*—McCall (1997)

20. Owens, R. G., & Valesky, T. C. (2022). *Organizational behavior in education: Leadership and school reform* (12th ed.). Pearson Education.

21. *ibid.*—McCall (1997)

22. *ibid.*—Rothwell (2005)

23. Gordon, S. P., & Niemiec, J. (2020). State assessment for principal licensure: Traditional, transitional, or transformative? A policy brief. *International Journal of Educational Leadership Preparation, 15*(1), 107–125. https://www.icpel.org/uploads/1/5/6/2/15622000/ijelp_volume_15_spring_2020.pdf

24. Thomas, J. G. (2011). *Exploring succession leadership training for continuity of leadership in selected K–12 school jurisdictions in Alberta* (Publication No. 3674163) [Doctoral dissertation, University of Phoenix]. ProQuest Dissertations and Theses Global.

25. Zepeda, S. J., Bengtson, E., & Parylo, O. (2012). Examining the planning and management of principal succession. *Journal of Educational Administration, 50*(2), 136–158. https://doi.org/10.1108/09578231211210512

26. Riddick, F. P. (2009). *What is your bench strength? An exploration of succession planning in three large school districts in a southeastern state* (Publication No. 3395265) [Doctoral dissertation]. ProQuest Dissertations and Theses Global.

27. Griggs, D. M., Kochan, R. K., & Reames, E. H. (2017). Investigating the benefits of a school/industry partnership focused on overcoming the skills gap and fostering student success. *Southeast Journal of Educational Administration, 17*(2), 72–87.

Kochan, F. K., & Griggs, D. (Eds.). (2020). *Creating partnerships that work: A guide for practice and research*. Information Age Publishing.

Chapter 6

An Overview of Talent Management

Management of talent will constitute the "heart" of succession planning, because the development and mentoring of individuals are facets with which senior leaders have direct and measurable impact. Additionally, regardless of the *potential* of the individuals identified, without targeted and specific development and proper mentoring, the chances of success are greatly lessened.

The following chapters in this section will include an avoidance of generic training, a greater examination of targeted and specific development, and a discussion of the importance of formal and informal mentoring. With appropriately managed development, there is never a reason to have a lack of qualified individuals prepared to assume positions of greater authority *at every level of the organization*!

HAVING THE "RIGHT STUFF"

As cited previously, Morgan McCall discussed the fallacies in the business world with the belief that natural born leaders simply had the "right stuff." Those who succeeded and excelled had it, and those who faltered were misidentified and truly did not have the right stuff.[1] Unfortunately, this mind-set is still often seen among school leaders. Worse yet, some believe—erroneously—that identification of those with the right stuff should solely belong to one person, often the current principal.[2]

The concepts and ideas presented in this set of chapters do not need to be reiterated. Therefore, the primary question now must be, what to do with those who have been identified and have the *potential*. But, potential is a very dangerous word; it is not what is or what will be; rather, what might be, what could be. Unfortunately, there are times in which individuals do not live up to their fullest potential.

FOSTERING SUCCESS

While there is never any guarantee that an individual will be successful in a given situation, proactive steps must be taken to provide him or her with all of the requisite experiences and ensuring credentials are commensurate. Therefore, those in leadership positions, and especially those in senior-level positions, must have a growth mind-set and view leadership development as an integral part of their jobs.[3] Even beyond a mere component of the job, the most successful ones believe there is a moral imperative to ensure others are prepared to assume positions of greater responsibility.[4]

Leadership development must be an integral part of the culture at all levels of the organization. Furthermore, the process must be systematic and purposeful.[5] Specific individuals need to be assigned for leadership development, but executive-level leaders must be a part of the entire succession-planning process.[6] For a non-education example, the leadership development program at General Electric during the tenure of Jack Welch was used as a laboratory to have promising talent address actual problems facing the company, and then present their recommendations directly to the board of directors.[7]

REAL-WORLD PROBLEMS

Solving real-world issues through problem-based and project-based learning is an important component. However, to ensure suitability for future positions, development must be based on the individual's unique needs and skill set. For example, a decent-sized school district already had an established leadership program. Individuals had to complete a year-long program and have met all of the requirements before being added to the specific pool and thus being eligible for promotion.

Despite having specific and detailed requirements and ensuring each individual had met a minimum time in a position before being eligible for a promotion, the director of leadership development uncovered a major issue with newly promoted principals. Despite having a minimum of four years' experience as an assistant principal, and having completed the year-long development program, many of the new principals did not have experience or even the skills to manage the school budget.

After examining the issue further, it was discovered that a change in the principal evaluation meant that any budgetary issue was potential cause for removal. Therefore, principals became so guarded with the budgets that they did not even include their own assistant principals involved in the process. Unfortunately then, many of those assistant principals were promoted and had no knowledge or experience with the process and required substantial remediation for a skill set they should have already had. Targeted development plans are one solution to the problem.

There are examples of successful development programs being implemented by school district officials. For example, researchers Phyllis Durden, Jorge Izquierdo, and James Williams reviewed a development program implemented in the New York City Schools. Applicants were rated using multiple-prong instruments, the most promising were selected for entry into the program, and then based on experiences and assessments, each person was provided with an individualized development plan. No two plans were similar, as each candidate had identified experiences to develop knowledge and skills.[8]

BENEFITS OF TARGETED DEVELOPMENT

Having prior and appropriate leadership experiences is a source of confidence and influences the efficacy of newly appointed leaders.[9] Having robust processes and individualized development programs is especially important for those being prepared to become principal, as the role of assistant principal greatly varies by setting,[10] and there is substantial ambiguity for expectations and determinations of success.[11] The avoidance of generic training and greater discussion of targeted and specific development will be detailed in subsequent chapters.

While the authors from the Gallup Corporation specify to focus only building upon strengths and ignoring weaknesses,[12] most other researchers recommend addressing limitations and weaknesses. Early exposure to weaknesses and limitations can be a tremendous opportunity for skills development,[13] although care must be taken to ensure the skill development is aligned to future needs. Preparing a new leader to create a master schedule only using paper is probably not the most appropriate development with the proliferation of software-based options today.

Albeit a morbid consideration, having a proper succession plan in place with multiple individuals who have the requisite credentials and experience is very beneficial and helpful to an organization when a current leader is tragically lost.[14] Although there is always a possibility of an individual failing in a new position, having no plan is a far greater risk, especially because a search process may be timely and expensive, and there is no guarantee of finding a suitable person in a needed timeframe.[15]

IDEAL DEVELOPMENT

So, what are some characteristics of effective targeted development? Business authors specify that a combination of job rotation, special assignments, classroom training, and real-life exposure is needed for effective targeted development.[16] Adaptations for an educational setting are certainly needed for effective development. While an individual does not necessarily have to be an English, math, and science teacher to evaluate teachers in those disciplines, he or she does need the understanding of the pedagogical aspects to ensure those teachers are being effective.

Special assignments in an education setting should include exposure to those facets with which a person does not have experience. Even in aspects with which a person is familiar, there is a tremendous difference between observing student discipline and participating in handling it. Those special assignments must be determined based on the needs of the individual. Assigning a person to assist with coordinating dismissal will not be effective if he or she had spent six months assisting a transportation administrator during an internship.

Classroom-based activities are not limited to a degree-seeking program. Regular professional development is needed in every situation.[17] As mentioned in the prior chapter, having the proper credentials is a prerequisite, and a minimum of a master's degree from an accredited institution is needed for state certification.[18] The experiences must then be augmented through district-and school-based classroom training.

With a quality succession plan, individuals will have greater marketability, and some will leave to pursue opportunities with other organizations.[19] Rather than lament the loss of talented individuals, pride should be taken knowing that the organization has an effective program and is producing individuals with the knowledge, skills, and dispositions. Business author Noel Tichy cited correspondence with the leadership director of Procter and Gamble, who took great pride in the fact previous employees were now in executive-level positions with more than 100 major corporations.[20]

MENTORING

Along with the focus on targeted and specific development, there must also be robust and effective mentoring opportunities. Mentoring must include a combination of formal and informal opportunities. Effective leaders need to be cognizant of the fact formal programs do not and cannot meet all of the needs of new and aspiring leaders, and therefore they will seek informal opportunities. Informal mentoring must be part of the culture of the organization.[21]

Throughout each chapter the importance of organizational culture is stressed; however, an extra focus on culture is needed for mentoring. Mentoring is a time-consuming process and can easily become an ineffective process if viewed only as a perfunctory task.[22] Problems and disparity among mentor and protégé are often reasons individuals seek informal mentors to compensate for the lack of a quality formal mentor.[23]

Therefore, care must be taken to ensure formal program are structured as effectively as possible. Although there are typically limits on the timeframe a mentoring relationship can last—often two years is the general rule[24]—programs must be structured to provide a foundation greater than the minimum. For example, Sharon Brittingham studied succession issues in a fast-growing school district in Delaware. The assistant superintendent recognized the future needs, and in establishing a rigorous process instituted a two-year rotating mentorship program.[25]

TRUST

No matter how well structured a formal mentoring program may be, there will always be issues and reasons for individuals to seek informal mentoring opportunities.[26] This is why culture is so important, and specifically development of trust; trust is the preeminent factor in all mentoring relationships.[27] Depending upon the setting, the mentor may be in a position to evaluate the protégé, which can be an issue, but if there is a high level of trust, then the relationship may be fruitful.[28]

Trust is the foundation to mentoring, not the goal. There are other aspects of effective mentoring relationships to consider. Flexibility and adaptability are key considerations, especially for school leaders who cannot always manage stringent and defined times for meetings.[29] Commitment from both, as well as a development-focused mind-set, is imperative for success. Benefits and weaknesses for formal and informal mentoring will be discussed in greater depth in Chapter 9.

CONCLUDING THOUGHTS

The purpose of this chapter was to provide an overview of the development and mentoring process for succession planning. While some examples have been cited or provided, any development program must be designed with the specific needs of the individual, but also for the proper organizational fit

Use the Likert-type responses to answer each question.

1. To what extent is there a defined pool process or other procedure to ensure aspiring leaders have the proper credential and minimum experience?
[ ] *Established*   [ ] *Implementing*   [ ] *Conceptual*   [ ] *None*

2. To what extent do **all** job descriptions and recruitment materials have clearly defined minimum criteria (e.g., years of experience, education level, additional requirements)?
[ ] *Established*   [ ] *Implementing*   [ ] *Conceptual*   [ ] *None*

3. To what extent are procedures in place to ensure all candidates have met or exceeded qualifications before a position is offered?
[ ] *Established*   [ ] *Implementing*   [ ] *Conceptual*   [ ] *None*

4. To what extent do identified leadership candidates have individualized development plans?
[ ] *Established*   [ ] *Implementing*   [ ] *Conceptual*   [ ] *None*

5. To what extent are current leaders held accountable for growth of subordinates?
[ ] *Established*   [ ] *Implementing*   [ ] *Conceptual*   [ ] *None*

6. To what extent are added special assignments, internships, and organization-based classroom learning used to foster knowledge and skill development?
[ ] *Established*   [ ] *Implementing*   [ ] *Conceptual*   [ ] *None*

7. To what extent is mentoring an ingrained aspect of the organizational culture?
[ ] *Established*   [ ] *Implementing*   [ ] *Conceptual*   [ ] *None*

8. To what extent are formal mentoring programs used?
[ ] *Established*   [ ] *Implementing*   [ ] *Conceptual*   [ ] *None*

9. To what extent are leaders encouraged to mentoring aspiring leaders informally?
[ ] *Established*   [ ] *Implementing*   [ ] *Conceptual*   [ ] *None*

10. To what extent does the organization have an individual or entity responsible for coordinating mentoring and development?
[ ] *Established*   [ ] *Implementing*   [ ] *Conceptual*   [ ] *None*

Figure 6.1.   Development and Mentoring Best Practices Checklist

with the unique culture. While many corporate leaders attempted to duplicate General Electric's success with its leadership development program, the most successful emulation was found in those companies in which the executives structured programs to fit the specific culture.[30]

Ensuring the organizational values are perpetuated is a primary focus on the development of future leaders. Each must have the combination of the requisite experiences and credentials to be successful. Development must be targeted and specific to each individual, and the conditions for formal and informal mentoring must be present. To provide a baseline for leaders to examine current organization, Figure 6.1 contains a rudimentary checklist for best practices in development and mentoring.

CHAPTER REFERENCES

1. McCall, M. W., Jr. (1997). *High flyers: Developing the next generation of leaders*. Harvard Business School Press.

2. Hengel, R. I. (2006). *Leadership capacity: Planning for leadership succession in schools* (Publication No. 304719536) [Master's thesis, Royal Roads University]. ProQuest Dissertations and Theses Global.

3. Tichy, N. M. (2014). *Succession: Mastering the make-or-break process of leadership transition*. Portfolio/Penguin.

4. Smeltzer, C. H. (2002). Succession planning. *Journal of Nursing Administration, 32*(12), 615.

5. Conger, J. A., & Fulmer, R. M. (2003). Developing your leadership pipeline. *Harvard Business Review, 81*(12), 76–84.

6. Rothwell, W. J. (2005). *Effective succession planning: Ensuring leadership continuity and building talent from within* (3rd ed.). AMACOM.

7. *ibid.*—Tichy (2014)

8. Durden, P. C., Izquierdo, J., & Williams, J. A. (2008). Out of the ashes: Building leadership and sustainability amid the chaos. *AASA Journal of Scholarship and Practice, 5*(3), 47–52.

9. Santacrose, D. M. (2016). *A mixed-methods study on the perceived role of novice assistant principals and the essence of their lived experience* (Publication No. 10246160) [Doctoral dissertation, Florida Gulf Coast University]. ProQuest Dissertations and Theses Global.

10. Oleszewsku, A., Shoho, A., & Barnett, B. (2012). The development of assistant principals: A literature review. *Journal of Educational Administration, 50*(3), 264–286. https://doi.org/10.1108/09578231211223301

11. Hausman, C., Nebeker, A., McCreary, J., & Donaldson, G. (2002). The worklife of the assistant principal. *Journal of Educational Administration, 40*(2/3), 136–157. https://doi.org/10.1108/09578230210421105

12. Clifton, D. O., & Harter, J. K. (2003). *Investing in strengths*. Gallup. https://strengthszone.com/wp-content/uploads/2016/01/Investing-In-Strengths.pdf

(Reprinted from *Positive organizational scholarship: Foundations of a new discipline*, pp. 111–121, by K. S. Cameron, J. K. Dutton, & R. S. Quinn, Eds., 2003, Berrett-Koehler Publishers).

13. *ibid.*—Conger & Fulmer (2003)

14. Gurchiek, K. (2015, November 15). *Don't leave succession planning to chance.* Society for Human Resource Management. https://www.shrm.org/hrdisciplines/orgempdev/articles/pages/leadership-manyorganizations-fail-at-succession-planning.aspx

15. Behn, B. K., Riley, R. A., Jr., & Yang, Y. (2005). The value of an heir apparent in succession planning. *Corporate Governance, 13*(2), 168–177.

16. *ibid.*—Conger & Fulmer (2003)

17. Korthagen, F. (2017). Inconvenient truths about teacher learning: Towards professional development 3.0. *Teachers and Teaching, 23*(4), 387–405. https://doi.org/10.1080/13540602.2016.1211523

18. Gordon, S. P., & Niemiec, J. (2020). State assessment for principal licensure: Traditional, transitional, or transformative? A policy brief. *International Journal of Educational Leadership Preparation, 15*(1), 107–125. https://www.icpel.org/uploads/1/5/6/2/15622000/ijelp_volume_15_spring_2020.pdf

19. Gothard, S., & Austin, M. J. (2013). Leadership succession planning: Implications for nonprofit human services organizations. *Administration in Social Work, 37*(3), 272–285. https://doi.org/10.1080/03643107.2012.684741

20. *ibid.*—Tichy (2014)

21. Parfitt, C. M., & Rose, A. L. (2020). Informal mentoring for aspiring school leaders: A phenomenological study. *Mentoring and Tutoring: Partnership in Learning, 28*(3), 278–294. https://doi.org/10.1080/13611267.2020.1778837

22. Holt, D. T., Markova, G., Dhaenens, A. J., Marler, L. E., & Heilmann, S. G. (2016). Formal or informal mentoring: What drives employees to seek informal mentors? *Journal of Management Issues, 28*(1–2), 67–82.

23. *ibid.*

24. Ettore, B. (1993, February). Who is this person? Focus on the number two. *Management Review*, 10–15.

25. Brittingham, S. L. (2009). Principal succession in a fast-growing district. *School Administrator, 66*(11), 22–25. https://aasa.org/SchoolAdministratorArticle.aspx?id=10144

26. James, J. M., Rayner, A., & Bruno, J. (2015). Are you my mentor? New perspectives and research on informal mentorship. *Journal of Academic Librarianship, 41*(2015), 532–539.

27. Zepeda, S. J., Bengtson, E., & Parylo, O. (2012). Examining the planning and management of principal succession. *Journal of Educational Administration, 50*(2), 136–158.

28. Collins-Camargo, C., & Kelly, M. J. (2006). Supervisor as informal mentor. *Clinical Supervisor, 25*(1–2), 127–146. https://doi.org/10.1300/j001v25n01_09

29. Ragins, B. R. (2016). From the ordinary to the extraordinary: High-quality mentoring relationships at work. *Organizational Dynamics, 45*(3), 228–244.

30. *ibid.*—Tichy (2014)

Chapter 7

Avoiding Generic Training

As mentioned in the previous chapter, effective development must be targeted and specific to the individual. Unfortunately, such programs are usually exceptions in educational organizations. For myriad reasons—lack of time, lack of funding, lack of personnel, and overlapping job responsibilities, for example—leadership development is often relegated to a task completed when needed or just to meet state-level requirements.[1]

Unfortunately, such trends in education are common. Best practices adopted by other disciplines are often in place for 20 to 30 years before the same practices are incorporated into educational organizations. Succession planning is a prime example.[2] Even at a micro level, business authors had written about targeted development before the turn of the 21st century.[3] Although targeted development is the goal, the opposite must be discussed.

GENERIC MANAGEMENT AND LEADERSHIP TRAINING

Before delving into the reasons to avoid generic training, the concept must first be defined. Generic training is a "one-size-fits-all" viewpoint that providing courses or programs pertaining to general leadership for all participants is sufficient for development. Mandating all aspiring leaders to complete such courses or programs without consideration of the future skills needed is ineffective and inefficient.[4]

An important distinction must be made between generic training and requisite training. Requisite or required training would constitute the minimum acceptable level of training and is often the benchmark to meet specific requirements, such as a master's degree for initial leadership certification or post-master's coursework for advanced certification. For an educational organization then to require aspiring leaders to complete additional courses that cover the same material is a waste of time and resources. Such coursework would only be appropriate if an individual needed greater exposure to the concepts.

A GOOD STEWARD OF FINITE RESOURCES

A counterargument is often made that individualized development is too costly or time prohibitive. However, when indirect and other hidden, as well as direct costs are calculated into replacing an individual, with the lost time from several individuals including supervisors, among other factors, the true cost of replacing an employee may be equivalent to 90% of the total salary if the process is handled extremely well and exceed 200% of the total salary if handled poorly.[5]

Corporate boards of directors and even boards of trustees/regents for colleges and universities often assert their most important function is to select and evaluate the chief executive, yet paradoxically, only six out of 25 private institutions of higher education surveyed by Melissa Klein and Raintry Salk had a succession plan. Of the six, most were simply procedures to conduct a nationwide search.[6] As equally perplexing considering the substantial literature pertaining to succession planning in the business sector, as of 2015, only 42% of 505 international corporations had any succession plan with an additional 33% in various stages of completion.[7]

The financial concern is elevated with executive-level positions. The greater the position, the greater cost if a person does not succeed, especially in a chief executive position.[8] In any educational organization, resources are precious commodities and cannot be wasted. Being a good steward of public funds is an important component to success as a school leader.[9] As provided in Case Study 7.1 (see Figure 7.1), two contrasting approaches to leadership development in school districts are examined. The merits will be addressed throughout the chapter.Figure 7.1. A Tale of Two Systems

"SHOW ME THE MONEY!"

The oft repeated phrase has been part of the lexicon since the 1996 premiere of the movie *Jerry Maguire*.[10] While there is comedic value in uttering the phrase, for many educational leaders the phrase "do more with less" is commonly heard instead. Though few know the original attribution of the quote is from a 1938 book by R. Buckminster Fuller.[11] But how much money is enough? There is no formula, and every organization will be different.

One important note is that just because funds are available, does not mean money should be spent frivolously. There are diminishing returns with

Case Study 7.1

A Tale of Two Systems

The Lincoln School System (LSS) has had a leadership development program in place for over 20 years. The founding director had been a successful principal with over 10 years' experience before accepting the challenge to develop the program for LSS.

A robust pool process was developed for potential assistant principals, and a separate process for current assistant principals to be prepared to assume a head role. Later, a year-long mentoring program for new principals was added. Then, a pool process for curriculum specialists. A program for senior-level, central-office positions is being developed.

Each pool process has stringent application requirements with a minimum amount of time in the current position, written assessments by multiple supervisors, documented annual success on the district evaluation, and completion of the appropriate state-level certification program at an accredited institution of higher education. A person must be accepted in the requisite pool before being eligible to apply for the next.

For example, many experienced teachers who held quasi-leadership positions as department or grade-level chair and have state certification in educational leadership must complete the year-long program for curriculum specialist before being eligible to apply for the assistant principal pool.

Once accepted into a cohort, there are mandatory evening classes at the district office held every other week, plus reading and electronic assignments. There is no deviation for prior experience or needs, and participants often complain that assignments are simply case studies and concepts that were covered in graduate-level courses. Update classes are held for those who have been in the pool for three years or more.

The leadership development program is very costly to the district, which is considered to be located in a wealthy area. The stringent and elaborate processes have been cited as a reason why talented teachers have sought opportunities elsewhere to become administrators sooner.

In contrast, the Washington School District (WSD) recently assigned a human resources administrator oversight for district leadership development. The individual was a principal in the past but former colleagues speak among themselves that the administrator was not qualified for the position, did not have the

Figure 7.1. A Tale of Two Systems

> experience, but maintained a close personal friendship with the deputy superintendent.
>
> Pool processes were previously established for principals and assistant principals; however, those with political connections have been known to bypass the processes completely. The processes were minimalistic, and only consisted of essays for leadership standards and interviews with panels of current principals and assistant principals.
>
> Training is held inconsistently for current administrators, with participants often citing a lack of substance when development sessions are held. A frequent assertion from the senior-level leaders is that "money is tight" and everyone has "such full plates" that mandating additional training is difficult.
>
> WSD is located in a community considered to be above the median income level for the state, but not considered wealthy. Despite the lack of professional development for current and aspiring leaders, members of the school board have described the central office as "bloated" and "far too top-heavy."
>
> While each district has inherent flaws, which setting would be preferred for a new superintendent? Throughout the remaining pages of the chapter, additional information will be provided to frame a perspective for appropriate targeted and specific development that is also fiscally responsible.

Figure 7.1. Continued

investment in any program.[12] The Lincoln School System from Case Study 7.1 had a very robust program with many positive attributes, multiple measures of talent, mandatory formal mentoring, and unwavering requirements. However, all of the training and development were generic. Very minimal aspects of the year-long program contained new information for the participants; they were often reteaching concepts from state-mandated master's degree programs.

Whereas in the case study, senior leaders from the Washington School District asserted the funds were not available, or rather, there was no importance placed in developing future leaders. Considering the comments from school board members about fiscal mismanagement, appropriate funds could presumably be located given the appropriate effort and the requisite level of support from the senior leaders.

Funding in education is always a contentious topic and is often cited as a reason for inequitable outcomes among schools because of varying levels of preparedness of teachers.[13] Regardless of the institution size, an appropriate level of funding for succession planning must be devoted. Business authors often assign the responsibility for underscoring the importance of succession planning to human resources officials.[14] Unfortunately, there is often a disconnect between strategic initiatives and leadership development.[15]

Although retention will be discussed in chapters 10, 11, and 12, it is important to note that retaining current employees has a far greater return on investment than recruiting new talent.[16] To retain quality individuals, transparency throughout the entire process is needed.[17] Additionally, dedicated and specific responsibility must be assigned for leadership development,[18] and every leader in the organization must be held responsible for developing the skill sets of others under his or her supervision.[19]

FIX IT OR SCRAP IT?

Considering very few educational organizations have quality succession-planning processes in place, what should be done with current—generally ineffective—programs? Expanding and strengthening existing programs is an appropriate start.[20] Rarely is a professional development program so terrible that it must be discarded completely and recreated. Additionally, success is not an immediate outcome, and the processes must become embedded into the organizational culture. The Japanese concept of *kaizen*—continuous changes through small, incremental steps—is an appropriate viewpoint.[21]

The Lincoln School System would have a clear advantage over the Washington School District from the case study, because robust programs were already in place, the extensive pool processes were part of the culture, and substantial resources were being spent on development. Changes need to be made to refocus the classroom sessions on new information for the participants and establishing individualized development programs. Location-based and other external opportunities need to be added as well.

A greater amount of work will be needed for the Washington School District; however, there are components already in place. The pool processes for principal and assistant can be revamped to include multiple measures of identification, dispositional assessments, and quality-control assurances. Considering there is a current administrator responsible for leadership development, the procedures are not beginning "from scratch." After entry into the program, targeted and specific development plans can be created with opportunities for the individuals to develop the knowledge, skills, and dispositions.

DEDICATED RESPONSIBILITY

Although mentioned several times in this chapter, ensuring a specific person or entity has authority and responsibility for leadership development is one of William Rothwell's 15 points to effective succession planning.[22] While business authors ascribe the responsibility for warning executives to human-resources officials, educational organizations do not always share consistent organizational structures, and depending upon the size of the organization, all of the major responsibilities may be entrusted to a limited number of individuals. Therefore, flexibility is important; there just needs to be a person responsible.

When having a dedicated person, small- size and rural districts are often at a disadvantage.[23] The issue can be that too few people "wear too many hats" or that there is a real or perceived lack of funding.[24] But having an individual dedicated to overseeing development does not mean that the person cannot have other job responsibilities. In a very small district, the superintendent himself may be the one responsible for development. The most important point to underscore is the enculturation of leadership development, which must then become a sustainable part of the organizational culture.[25]

SUSTAINING A SUSTAINABLE CULTURE

While most leaders presumably hope to be in a position for considerable time, there is never a guarantee. Without describing the process as succession planning, Michael Fullan addressed the need for a leader to plan for his or her departure from the very first day in the position.[26] His focus was creating a sustainable process to ensure perpetuation of a positive culture. Creating a sustainable culture must be unique to each setting, and perpetuation needs to be specific to the needs of the individuals being prepared for greater positions.

Business consultant Noel Tichy contended that a lack of a successful leadership pipeline—primarily focused on CEO succession—was indicative of an unhealthy organizational culture.[27] He further opined that, barring the rare exception in which an outsider is needed to bring new ideas and correct problems, there is never a reason for an organization not to have qualified individuals to replace an executive. Development must be specific to the needs of those individuals in the "horse race" as he described.

Unfortunately, Tichy also believed that executive succession was ineffective a majority of the time. Too many organizations had succession plans but were overly focused on technical aspects to the exclusion of cultural and political concerns.[28] Other business authors have asserted that organizations had ineffective plans because of the delimitations only to executive or senior positions.[29] The ineffective plans including a lack of senior involvement and a failure to address all levels of the organization were directly contradictory to William Rothwell's components for effective succession planning.[30]

THE POLITICS OF EDUCATION

Tichy considered politics to be one of the three intertwined aspects to consider,[31] and unfortunately "navigating the waters" of politics in education is unavoidable in leadership positions. However, using an appropriate succession plan can mitigate political factors, especially in the use of 360-degree assessments[32] and by providing an open and transparent process for all stakeholders.[33]

The concept of 360-degree assessments were previously discussed in Chapter 3, but it is worth noting that mitigating biases in assessment is important. Also, the results of assessments must be used in creating individualized development plans for candidates. Clearly though, senior leaders must expend some political capital to ensure robust systems are in place. From a business standpoint, delaying succession planning and targeted individual development in particular because of day-to-day operations or other deadlines is not an acceptable practice.[34]

Finally, an open and transparent process is vital for stakeholders at all levels of the organization.[35] Input from all groups of stakeholders is imperative, including support staff and external members.[36] Expectations for positions must be outlined clearly and based on future needs, not changed based on politics to suit a narrow set of candidates. Success can never be ensured; however, by engaging all stakeholders, unique aspects of subcultures can be considered and will help ensure a leadership candidate is best suited for the position.

CONCLUDING THOUGHTS

Whether through a lack of time, funding, or a host of other issues, targeted and specific development is rare in education. While there may be greater upfront costs, the possibilities for long-term success of the organization will be greater if a robust system for leadership development is enacted. Proactive, as opposed to reactive, is always going to be a better approach, especially for targeted and specific leadership development.

Regardless of how much time and how many resources are spent on generic training, individuals will not be as appropriately prepared as they will through a targeted and specific program. Most generic leadership training is often repetitious for the participants and merely addresses components learned through formal degree programs. Fortunately, for most organizations, existing structures and programs can be modified and changed to meet the needs of the future leaders.

To meet the needs of the organization, specific and dedicated responsibility must be established. While having an individual or even a department dedicated to leadership development is ideal, smaller organizations may not be able to have a person assigned only to leadership development. Regardless of the size of the organization, there must be a specific person or people with responsibility for ensuring proper leadership development, and those individuals must be held accountable.

Beyond dedicated responsibility, other cultural shifts must occur for leadership development to become a sustainable initiative. Current leaders must have an awareness of succession planning and take actionable steps to enculturate leadership development as a focus in the organization at every level. Although the political aspects of leadership succession will always be present, a positive organizational culture and use of best practices will minimize biases and allow for transparency. While the focus of this chapter was avoiding generic training, greater specificity for targeted and specific development will be discussed in the next.

CHAPTER REFERENCES

1. Parfitt, C. M. (2017). Perceptions of succession planning in four Florida school districts: A mixed-method study. *Southeast Journal of Educational Administration, 17*(2), 88–115.

2. Neefe, D. O. (2009). *Succession planning in a two-year technical college system* (Publication No. 3360378) [Doctoral dissertation, University of Minnesota]. ProQuest Dissertations and Theses Global.

3. Beeson, J. (1998). Succession planning: Building the management corps. *Business Horizons, 41*(5), 61–66.

4. Conger, J. A., & Fulmer, R. M. (2003). Developing your leadership pipeline. *Harvard Business Review, 81*(12), 76–84.

5. Allen, D. G. (2006). *Retaining talent: A guide to analyzing and managing employee turnover* (SHRM Foundation's effective practice guidelines series). Society for Human Resources Management.

6. Klein, M. F., & Salk, R. J. (2013). Presidential succession planning: A qualitative study in private higher education. *Journal of Leadership and Organizational Studies, 20*(3) 335–345. https://doi.org/10.1177/1548051813483836

7. Gurchiek, K. (2015, November 15). *Don't leave succession planning to chance*. Society for Human Resource Management. https://www.shrm.org/hrdisciplines/orgempdev/articles/pages/leadership-manyorganizations-fail-at-succession-planning.aspx

8. McCall, M. W., Jr. (1997). *High flyers: Developing the next generation of leaders*. Harvard Business School Press.

9. National Policy Board for Educational Administration. (2015). *Professional standards for educational leaders*. Author. https://ccsso.org/sites/default/files/2017-10/ProfessionalStandardsforEducationalLeaders2015forNPBEAFINAL.pdf

10. Crowe, C. (Director/Writer), & Brooks, J. L. (Producer). (1996). *Jerry Maguire* [Film]. TriStar Pictures.

11. Fuller, R. B. (1938). *Nine chains to the moon*. Anchor Books.

12. McFadyen, M. A., & Cannella, A. A. (2004). Social capital and knowledge creation: Diminishing returns of the number and strength of exchange relationships. *Academy of Management Journal, 47*(5), 735–746. https://doi.org/10.5465/20159615

13. Cuenca, A., & Nichols, J. R., Jr. (2019). Framing teacher education: An analysis of the comprehensive educator equity plans of 16 state education agencies. *New Educator, 15*(1), 1–17, https://doi.org/10.1080/1547688X.2018.1424980

14. *ibid.*—Gurchiek (2015)

15. *ibid.*—Neefe (2009)

16. Chavez, J. (2011). The case for succession planning. *Strategic Finance, 92*(8), 15–16.

17. *ibid.*—Beeson (1998)

18. Rothwell, W. J. (2005). *Effective succession planning: Ensuring leadership continuity and building talent from within* (3rd ed.). AMACOM.

19. *ibid.*—Beeson (1998)

20. *ibid.*—Neefe (2009)

21. Owens, R. G., & Valesky, T. C. (2022). *Organizational behavior in education: Leadership and school reform* (12th ed.). Pearson Education.

22. *ibid.*—Rothwell (2005)

23. Zepeda, S. J., Bengtson, E., & Parylo, O. (2012). Examining the planning and management of principal succession. *Journal of Educational Administration, 50*(2), 136–158. https://doi.org/10.1108/09578231211210512

24. *ibid.*—Parfitt (2017)

25. Fullan, M. (2005). *Sustainable leadership*. Corwin Press.

26. *ibid.*

27. Tichy, N. M. (2014). *Succession: Mastering the make-or-break process of leadership transition*. Portfolio/Penguin.

28. *ibid.*

29. *ibid.*—Gurchiek (2015)

30. *ibid.*—Rothwell (2005)

31. *ibid.*—Tichy (2014)

32. *ibid.*—Parfitt (2017)

33. Meyer, M. J., Macmillan, R. B., & Northfield, S. (2009). Principal succession and its impact on teacher morale. *International Journal of Leadership in Education: Theory and Practice, 12*(2), 171–185. https://doi.org/10.1080/13603120802449660

34. *ibid.*—Tichy (2014)

35. *ibid.*—Meyer, Macmillan, & Northfield (2009)

36. Emira, M. (2013). Support staff leadership: Opportunities and challenges. *Leadership, 9*(1), 23–41. https://doi.org/10.1177/1742715012455128

Chapter 8

Targeted and Specific Development

The focus of Chapter 7 was the avoidance of generic leadership training; this chapter will be centered on the specific aspects for targeted development and how to implement them effectively. Proper targeted and specific development is designed with a dual focus: to help the individual leadership candidate address aspects with which he or she has not had sufficient experience, and to ensure all of the candidates have the knowledge, skills, and dispositions to be effective and meet the future goals of the organization.

A TWO-FOLD APPROACH

Targeted and specific development must have a dual focus: the exposure and improvement of specific aspects that the candidate needs to learn or improve,[1] and enculturation or socialization into the position as a leader.[2] To achieve the dual purpose, input is needed from the candidate, and other appropriate individuals. After a comprehensive determination, detailed plans should be created with tasks and opportunities to have greater experience with each facet,[3] in conjunction with formal and informal mentoring.[4]

As mentioned in the previous chapter, a quality process is time consuming and labor intensive. However, if the process is handled appropriately, then the benefits far outweigh the costs. Although retention will be the focus of another section, an important facet to note is that properly trained and rewarded individuals are less likely to leave the organization.[5] While researchers over the past quarter century have shown that lack of support is a primary reason for teachers departing the field of education,[6] lack of input and upward mobility is a reason that promising leaders often leave an organization.[7]

Specific Improvement

Exposure to targeted facets and skill development needs to be established based on an individual candidate's prior experiences and needs. Futuristic considerations have been highlighted previously, and for myriad reasons. Preparing an individual to assume a position of greater authority often means that he or she will have to address unfamiliar tasks in a new position. Unfortunately, experiences and preparation are often assumed erroneously.[8]

For example, a school district in which principals are scrutinized closely pertaining to financial matters may inadvertently cause current principals to manage all fiscal matters directly with minimal or no input from others, including assistant principals. Then, when an individual is promoted to principal without having proper budgetary experience, he or she lacks the knowledge and skills needed to be successful, yet superiors presume he or she already had such exposure. Unintentionally, the new principal has been "set up for failure."

But, how does one begin to identify *future* needs? The answer was provided in the chapters for identification of talent. Job descriptions, strategic plans, and professional standards should be used as a basis from which to determine the knowledge, skills, and dispositions requisite for the position. There is, of course, the caveat that those documents are sufficient and reflect the true nature of the position. With any endeavor in leadership, professional judgment must be exercised.

Enculturation into a Position

Among the most frequently researched topics pertaining to succession planning in education is socialization or enculturation into a position.[9] There is a sufficient reason for the focus. Being prepared to serve as principal after having been a teacher is a dramatically different position. Whereas a teacher's schedule is fixed and for the most part, inflexible, a principal needs to exercise discretion and be superb at time management.[10] Success at one level does not guarantee success at another.

Enculturation is a process by which one becomes accustomed to the organizational culture and learns the organizational and positional responsibilities and expectations.[11] The challenges may be unique depending upon whether the individual promoted to a position of greater authority was employed in the same school district and even the same building. Supervising former peers can present specific challenges, especially if the individual had been a peer for a substantial amount of time.[12]

Role conflict is an important facet to discuss for assuming a position as a leader in any organization. The expectations of the myriad stakeholders can greatly vary from the stated job description and perception of the individual.[13] For example, if policy expectations are to return phone calls within 24 business hours, yet parents had been accustomed to receiving responses within a short period, a new principal can become disillusioned to learn that a parent had called the central office at 8:01 a.m. on Monday complaining that a voicemail left at 4:59 p.m. on Friday had not been returned.

Learning how to manage role conflict will be vital, and in some cases, new cultural norms and expectations will need to be established over time. Targeted and specific development is needed to assist new leaders in managing role conflict and provide enculturation into the position. Aspects for time and project management should be part of the targeted and specific development to ensure each is able to transition appropriately.

PRACTICAL APPLICATION

Now that specific improvement and enculturation have been defined, what steps are needed to enact the concepts in a leadership development program? Albeit a seemingly obvious aspect, a leadership development program needs to be in place. As was mentioned previously, specific authority and direct accountability are needed for oversight, coupled with executive-level involvement. Perhaps the most important facet is having a *future-oriented* vision.

The first step in practical application is to ensure there is alignment between what is assessed and what is important.[14] All materials from the position and job descriptions to the assessment instruments need to reflect the scope and parameters of the position effectively. Role conflict was mentioned previously, and it is incumbent on those responsible for assessment to ensure the true nature of the position is evaluated, not ancillary and ill-defined measures.

Preparation for Success

While there are examples throughout history of spontaneous successes, in most endeavors, quality preparation is needed; succession planning is no different. Independent of the size of the organization, determination of responsibility for leadership development must be established with clear authority and accountability.[15] Having the defined positions and with larger organizations, dedicated offices responsible is the first step in success.

Having the coherent and aligned materials and assessments is the second step. The old adage to "inspect what is expected" is apropos. However, as previously mentioned, there must be multiple perspectives used in creating the specific development plans. A direct supervisor may have drastically differing views on specific functions needed by an employee than do the subordinates or even external stakeholders who interact with the employee on a greater basis than does the supervisor.

A common "pitfall" for many organizations is role ambiguity in relation to colleagues and peers. A supervisor may be very clear in the expectations and requirements in a dyadic relationship.[16] However, if the colleagues and peers whose jobs are impacted by another do not view the individual as completing requisite tasks in a timeframe and manner they expect, there is a greater probability of role conflict.[17] The answer to avoiding role conflict is to have the input of all the apropos individuals and communicate the decisions and expectations effectively.

Assessing the Current Status

Knowing the requirements and skills needed for success is only part of the assessment. The individual's knowledge, skills, and dispositions must be assessed for a proper plan to be created. The plan should address any currents gaps, as well as prepare the individual for future needs.[18] One important aspect is that generic leadership and management training is not a substitute for targeted and specific development.[19]

For an effective plan, input is needed from the individual, and his or her supervisor at minimum. The goals need to be written with a combination or short-, medium-, and long-term outcomes. The purpose of the development plan is for the individual to acquire the knowledge, skills, and dispositions needed now and for future positions. Therefore, the plan needs to be clearly future oriented, and the mind-set is improvement, not fixing problems.[20]

Creating the Plan

Once all of the collective information is aggregated, job functions are clearly defined, and the specific needs of the individuals are identified, development plans need to be written and disseminated. Specific responsibility is needed for ensuring the plan is followed, and updates to executive leadership are paramount. While there is no "one-size-fits-all" approach, a leadership-development office or human-resources department can be responsible for maintaining records, but a specific person must have accountability for monitoring the plan.[21]

But, what needs to be included in the plan? There is no universal answer. Each plan must be created and designed for the unique individual. The format should be easy to follow and clearly list the goals, timeline for completion, and responsibility for oversight. A responsible office and individual should be custodians of the plan, and each needs to be reviewed by at least one senior-level executive.[22] See Figure 8.1 for a sample plan.

Name: Nicole Horn	Overall Responsible: Director, Leadership Development			
Position: Assistant Principal	Location: Seaside Elementary School			
Short-Term Goals (less than three months)				
Number	Skill	Task	Timeframe	Person Responsible
1	Instructional leadership Staff development	Learn to use the district observation tool effectively	End of September	Principal
2	Operational leadership Procedures	Create a new student dismissal plan	Two weeks prior to school start	Principal
Medium-Term Goals (three to six months)				
Number	Skill	Task	Timeframe	Person Responsible
3	Instructional leadership Student achievement	Independently conduct grade-level "data chats"	By the start of the second semester	Principal
4	Operational leadership School management	Become certified as the school's threat assessment representative	In 90 Days	Director, Safety and Security
Long-Term Goals (six months and greater)				
Number	Skill	Task	Timeframe	Person Responsible
5	Operational leadership Decision making	Learn to complete the district budget process independently	Before the start of the next academic year	Assistant Superintendent, Finance
6	Instructional leadership Student achievement	Learn to create a new strategic plan based on student data	Before the start of the next academic year	Principal

Figure 8.1. Sample Development Plan

Execution of the Plan

The best-created plans are meaningless unless implemented appropriately. While goals can feasibly be completed under the supervision of different individuals, there needs to be one person with responsibility for ensuring all goals of a subordinate are met.[23] Formal mentoring programs will be discussed in the next chapter; however, accountability is an important component for plan execution.

Implementing the plan should provide an opportunity for the leadership candidate to engage in the activities to the greatest extent possible. Presumably, without planned activities, the individual would not have otherwise had the opportunity to experience. In certain business vernacular, the experiences are often described as "stretch assignments," because the purpose is to have the individual complete work that is considered to be a stretch from usual job assignments.[24]

Although some supervisors are better than others with training opportunities, there should be a clear explanation pertaining to why tasks are accomplished and in the matter in which they should be completed. Supervisors need to be cognizant of the fact while conducting training opportunities, and remember the perspective of one who does not know the system and why certain aspects are handled in the ways in which they are.

Documentation of Results

As tasks are being completed, milestones need to be documented appropriately. Several of William Rothwell's 15 characteristics are evident in a proper development plan, including benchmarks and needs assessments, a developmental focus, dedicated responsibility, a systematic approach, and accountability to prepare future successors.[25] The documentation should serve as proof of the leadership candidate completing development and proper involvement of those responsible. During his time in leadership development at General Electric, Noel Tichy noted that the CEO was frequently involved in reviewing progress of subordinates at multiple levels.[26]

Documentation should be kept as proof an individual has completed targeted and specific development in the assigned facets by the leadership candidate and those responsible for overseeing leadership development. A portfolio documenting competence of the required facets is frequently used and an acceptable process for keeping track of progress.[27] With the myriad database systems in use today, a module for tracking development is a wise investment.[28]

Assessment of Results

Keeping track of development by itself is insufficient; the results must be analyzed continuously. Through the lens of William Rothwell's performance-management approach, there needs to be maintenance of success in a current position, analysis of past performance, and a substantial consideration for future impact.[29] Future considerations need to be forward thinking, and consideration for success should be two levels beyond the current setting.[30] Quite simply, preparing a new administrator to be an assistant principal is ineffective; he or she must be prepared to serve as principal and beyond.

Proper assessment must be multifaceted, just the same as talent identification. Regardless of how well structured an evaluation system is designed, elements of subjectivity will be present. From a purely quantitative perspective, interrater reliability greater than .8 is considered nearly perfect, but which means that the raters disagreed 20% of the time.[31] Plus, quantitative aspects are included because of measurability. But to measure for the sake of having documented assessment is ineffective. As Cecil Carter and Tom Valesky asked about a state-mandated school evaluation system, "is the ladder leaning against the wrong wall?"[32]

The use of multiple assessors helps mitigate—but never eliminate—bias, and it also can provide perspective on narrowing a focus to important factors.[33] Are truly important components being assessed, or were others included simply by the virtue of ease of measurement? In some cases, indirect measurements are helpful. If one school or central-office department has substantially greater turnover than others, is a quantitative measure needed to document poor organizational culture? This is why assessment must be comprehensive and focus on dispositions, in addition to the knowledge and skills necessary.

KNOWLEDGE, SKILLS, AND DISPOSITIONS

Throughout the chapters, a focus on the proper dispositions emerges, and with good reason. Dispositions are often the difference in success when all other factors are equal. Individuals with "poor" dispositions were far more likely to fail in a position.[34] However, exposure to proper standards-based dispositions can lead to improvement.[35] Within reason, dispositions can be taught, and those who were exposed to proper dispositions scored higher than all other groups who were not exposed to the dispositions.[36]

Proper dispositions aligned to standards must also be accompanied by the requisite knowledge and skills. Therefore, proper targeted and specific development must have components to address all three and through the lens of the specific organizational culture. An individual with the proper dispositions and skills can be severely limited in a position "because there is no substitute for having institutional knowledge."[37] However, strategic succession planning is a method to capture institutional or tacit knowledge.[38]

To overcome gaps in knowledge and attempt to minimize organizational instability through leadership succession, Linda Lee specified the importance of a planned transition, whether through planned continuity or planned discontinuity.[39] A plan is only effective if there are aspects to address the needed knowledge and organizational culture, as well as the skills and dispositions. But one important facet to highlight is that planned transition does equate to maintenance of the status quo; changes can certainly be made and strategic direction changed through planned discontinuity.

CONCLUDING THOUGHTS

Among the most important aspects for leadership development is the need for targeted and specific development. Regardless of how robust and comprehensive a program is designed, if the foci are generic leadership or management training, then the process will be ineffective. The two-pronged approach of addressing the need for knowledge, skills, and dispositions, as well as enculturation in the position and organization, are needed to be effective.

While the proper process is time consuming and labor intensive, the benefits outweigh the costs over time; improved retention of leaders and employees, lower human-resources costs, and fewer indirect costs are among the benefits. The old adage, "an ounce of prevention is worth a pound of cure" is very apropos. Even modest reductions in costs can be extremely beneficial for long-term fiscal health of the organization.

While there is no ubiquitous answer, determining the organizational needs; assessing an individual's knowledge, skills, and dispositions; creating a targeted and specific plan; executing the plan with fidelity and involving the requisite individuals; documenting the results appropriately; analyzing the results by involving multiple assessors including senior-level leaders; and using the results for continuous improvement are the necessary steps for ensuring those identified as future leaders are prepared to assume positions of greater authority. Within every phase, always consider the specific and unique organizational culture.

CHAPTER REFERENCES

1. Durden, P. C., Izquierdo, J., & Williams, J. L. (2008). Out of the ashes: Building leadership and sustainability amid the chaos. *AASA Journal of Scholarship and Practice*, *5*(3), 47–51.

2. Zepeda, S. J., Bengtson, E., & Parylo, O. (2012). Examining the planning and management of principal succession. *Journal of Educational Administration*, *50*(2), 136–158. https://doi.org/10.1108/09578231211210512

3. Brittingham, S. L. (2009). Principal succession in a fast-growing district. *School Administrator*, *66*(11), 22–25. https://aasa.org/SchoolAdministratorArticle.aspx?id=10144

4. Chavez, J. (2011). The case for succession planning. *Strategic Finance*, *92*(8), 15–16.

5. Beeson, J. (2000). Succession planning: Leading-edge practices: What the best companies are doing. *Across the Board*, *37*(2), 38–41.

6. Chase, B. (2000). Show us the money. *NEA Today*, *18*(7), 5.

Darling-Hammond, L. (2001). The challenge of staffing our schools. *Educational Leadership*, *58*(8), 12–17.

Ingersoll, R. M. (2001). Teacher turnover and teacher shortages: An organizational analysis. *American Education Research Journal*, *38*(3), 499–534.

Newberry, M., & Alsopp, Y. (2017). Teacher attrition in the USA: The relational elements in a Utah case study. *Teachers and Teaching: Theory and Practice*, *23*(8), 863–880. https://doi.org/10.1080/13540602.2017.1358705

7. McCall, M. W., Jr. (1997). *High flyers: Developing the next generation of leaders*. Harvard Business School Press.

8. Oleszewsku, A., Shoho, A., & Barnett, B. (2012). The development of assistant principals: A literature review. *Journal of Educational Administration*, *50*(3), 264–286. https://doi.org/10.1108/09578231211223301

9. Bengtson, E., Zepeda, S. J., & Parylo, O. (2013). School systems practices of controlling socialization during principal succession: Looking through the lens of organization socialization theory. *Educational Management Administration and Leadership*, *41*(2), 143–164. https://doi.org/10.1177/1741143212468344

10. Owens, R. G., & Valesky, T. C. (2022). *Organizational behavior in education: Leadership and school reform* (12th ed.). Pearson Education.

11. *ibid.*—Bengtson, Zepeda, & Parylo (2013)

12. Gallo, A. (2012, December 19). How to manage your former peers. *Harvard Business Review*. https://hbr.org/2012/12/how-to-manage-your-former-peer

13. *ibid.*—Owens & Valesky (2022)

14. Popham, W. J. (2000). *Modern educational measurement* (3rd ed.). Allyn and Bacon.

15. Rothwell, W. J. (2005). *Effective succession planning: Ensuring leadership continuity and building talent from within* (3rd ed.). AMACOM.

16. Wallis, N. C., Yammarino, F. J., & Feyerherm, A. (2011). Individualized leadership: A qualitative study of senior executive leaders. *Leadership Quarterly*, *22*(1), 182–206. https://doi.org/10.1016/j.leaqua.2010.12.015

17. *ibid.*—Owens & Valesky (2022)

18. *ibid.*—Rothwell (2005)

Conger, J. A., & Fulmer, R. M. (2003). Developing your leadership pipeline. *Harvard Business Review*, *81*(12), 76–84.

19. Beeson, J. (1998). Succession planning: Building the management corps. *Business Horizons*, *41*(5), 61–66.

20. Attributed to William W. Swann, PhD, former CEO, Leadership Coaching Institute.

21. *ibid.*—Durden, Izquierdo, & Williams (2008)
ibid.—Rothwell (2005)

22. *ibid.*

23. *ibid.*
ibid.—Beeson (1998)

24. *ibid.*—Chavez (2011)

25. *ibid.*—Rothwell (2005)

26. Tichy, N. M. (2014). *Succession: Mastering the make-or-break process of leadership transition*. Portfolio/Penguin.

27. Brown, G., & Irby, B. J. (1995). The portfolio: Should it also be used by administrators? *NASSP Bulletin*, *79*(570), 82–85. https://doi.org/10.1177/019263659507957014

28. Hawthorne, G. B., Novey, D. A., & Lewis, T. (2021). Using a framework to review and evaluate educational technology resources. *Southeast Journal of Educational Administration*, *20*(2), 154–168.

29. *ibid.*—Rothwell (2005)

30. *ibid.*—Beeson (1998)

31. Landis, J. R., & Koch, G. G. (1977). The measurement of observer agreement for categorical data. *Biometrics, 33*(1), 159–174. https://doi.org/10.2307/2529310

32. Carter, C. F., & Valesky, T. C. (2004, November). *Florida's accountability system: Is the ladder leaning against the wrong wall?* [Paper presentation]. Southern Regional Council on Educational Administration 45th Annual Conference, Raleigh, NC.

33. Brown, A., Inceoglu, I., & Lin, Y. (2017). Preventing rater biases in 360-degree feedback by forcing choice. *Organizational Research Methods, 20*(1), 121–148. https://doi.org/10.1177/1094428116668036

34. Martin, M. (2009). A case study of dispositions addressed in principal preparation programs as a transition into the internships. *International Journal of Educational Leadership Preparation, 4*(3). https://cnx.org/contents/jOpHfCd@1/A-Case-Study-of-Dispositions-A

35. LaPaglia, K. (2020). *Preservice teacher dispositions: A case study of changes during a teacher preparation program* (Publication No. 28314521) [Doctoral dissertation, Florida Gulf Coast University]. ProQuest Dissertations and Theses Global.

36. Parfitt, C. M., Rea, D. C., Carter, C. F., Wilkerson, J. R., Rose, A. L., & Valesky, T. C. (2019). Assessing leadership dispositions: Does explicit instruction matter? *Southeast Journal of Educational Administration, 19*(1), 67–77.

37. Attributed to Erica M. Vogt, M.Acc., p-resident and CEO of Foree Branch Consulting Services.

38. Lewis, L. T. (2013). *Capturing tacit knowledge through strategic succession planning: A phenomenological explication* (Publication No. 3557881) [Doctoral dissertation, Baker College]. ProQuest Dissertations and Theses Global.

39. Lee, L. C. (2015). School performance trajectories and the challenges for principal succession. *Journal of Educational Administration, 53*(2), 262–286. https://doi.org/10.1108/JEA-12-2012-0139

Chapter 9

Mentoring

Of the topics discussed, few are as expansive as mentoring. Many volumes have been written on myriad subtopics involving mentoring. However, the importance in succession planning cannot be overstated. For the purpose of discussion, this chapter will be divided into two major sections: (a) structured programs (i.e., formal mentoring) and (b) informal mentoring. Both are needed for quality succession planning.[1]

Before discussing the concept of mentoring, operationalized definitions are needed. A mentor is typically one who has greater skills, abilities, and experience. The purpose of having a mentor is for him or her to provide support and assistance with enculturation into the professional setting for another individual.[2] The person receiving guidance is defined as a mentee or protégé. In a broad sense, mentoring is not bound by age restrictions, and anyone who has an impact on the life of another can be considered a mentor.[3]

Before structured and informal mentoring are discussed, are there components across all forms of mentoring that are important? Absolutely! One singular component is needed for success in any mentoring situation . . . trust![4] In essence, trust is the foundation of mentoring, and mentoring is one of the most crucial components to talent management and quality succession planning; therefore, if talent management was previously defined as the "heart," then trust is arguably the "heartbeat" of succession planning.

Trust permits other qualities to emerge from a mentoring relationship: adaptability, flexibility, growth, and socialization.[5] An increase in job satisfaction and a long-term commitment to the organization are often positive benefits reported by protégés,[6] while mentors reported an increase in job satisfaction from helping others.[7] Additional benefits for mentors include exercising leadership abilities directly, as well as promoting their own job skills.[8]

STRUCTURED MENTORING PROGRAMS

Structured mentoring is any intentionally established program in which an employee is formally paired with another with defined roles and responsibilities.[9] Employee growth is a prime focus for mentoring, and the opportunity should benefit mentor and protégé.[10] As a developmental component, mentoring is a vital aspect for quality succession planning and must be planned appropriately.[11]

Most organizations have some type of structured mentoring program. However, the efficacy and success of such programs is debatable. Even well-structured programs that are implemented improperly are ineffective at best.[12] The issues are often a cause for individuals to seek informal mentors, which will be discussed in the second section of this chapter. Despite any challenges, structured programs are one of the most beneficial aspects for employee growth.[13] Benefits and challenges will be discussed for formal and informal processes.

Benefits of Structured Mentoring Programs

A structured program has one important aspect that is important for senior-level leadership: the process is completely controlled. If great care is given, mentors and protégés can be matched based on skill, ability, and even personality. While time can be a restraining factor, scheduling and requirements to meet with a protégé at assigned intervals can be positive aspects for both.[14] An effective mentor will learn as much from a protégé as he or she teaches.[15]

One of the most prominent, yet often unstated aspects of structured mentoring is the transmission of institutional knowledge—some authors have described the concept as tacit knowledge.[16] Because every organization is unique, every culture will be unique, and having a greater understanding and institutional knowledge will benefit an employee tremendously. To impart institutional knowledge, a mentor should be a collegial and collaborative coach.[17]

When a program is structured, financial incentives are one possible measure to reward mentors, but there are other equally important aspects that may have a positive impact on the organizational culture, such as release from certain duties and availability of developmental opportunities.[18] To ensure incentives and program structure are sufficient, mentoring must be integrated into strategic goals and promoted by human-resources personnel.[19] Proper mentoring cannot be an afterthought, or simply a program that exists to meet a minimum requirement.[20]

Strategic efforts encoded in a structured mentoring program can be used to foster and sustain a positive organizational culture and climate.[21] The all-important component of trust is not just vital for mentoring, but in general, and is indicative of a positive organizational culture.[22] Support also helps build confidence, improve competence, and increase self-efficacy, all of which assists the individual in overcoming isolation and anxiety from a new position.[23]

Challenges with Structured Mentoring Programs

Depending upon the relationship between mentor and protégé, an emotional connection could be a major limiting factor for supervisory effectiveness.[24] As was discussed in Chapter 2, a sense of personal loyalty and other non-job-related factors can be a hindrance in talent identification. The same is true in supervision. A "good" employee who has an emotional connection with a supervisor will be rated positively even with an admission of bias.

The hierarchical structure in an organization can also be a hindrance and prevent formation of effective mentoring relationships.[25] If an employee perceives the mentor in a superior position and his or her feedback could impact a performance evaluation, then the individual might not have the sense of trust in the mentor that is required for an effective relationship to develop.

Unfortunately, because there are often monetary incentives for serving as a mentor, individuals may volunteer simply because of the financial bonus, and then only put forth the minimal effort required to meet the organizational requirements. Limitations with structured mentoring arrangements are often a reason why individuals seek informal mentors to "fill the void" left by insufficient formal mentoring.[26]

INFORMAL MENTORING

While some individuals sought an informal mentor because of insufficient guidance from an assigned individual, the most frequently cited reasons are often convenience, level of trust, self-advocacy, and time.[27] Obviously, there is greater fluidity with an informal relationship. There are no defined roles or responsibilities, and no required format or allotment of time. In the simplest view, informal mentoring occurs when two individuals decide to work together to share knowledge with the purpose of improvement.[28]

Any mentoring relationship will only be successful and beneficial if there is a high level of trust, which is the preeminent factor for quality.[29] Successful informal mentoring relationships have an adaptive focus, are flexible, and are growth oriented.[30] Formation of informal relationships often occurs due to natural attraction of two individuals who have a desire to work together.[31] Particularly in smaller organizations, informal mentoring occurs out of necessity because of the need and limited scope and capacity of formal programs.[32]

Benefits of Informal Mentoring

Powerful, helpful, nonevaluative, and *supportive* are adjectives individuals have used to describe informal mentoring relationships. As a tool, informal mentoring can be used by leaders to build a positive culture by encouraging the development of informal relationships.[33] The mentor does not necessarily have to be in a superior position; he or she simply needs to be able to provide career advice, perspective, and support.[34]

The fact an individual may choose his or her own informal mentor is beneficial. Individuals often seek a mentor who is caring, fair, honest, and passionate. Quality informal mentors are approachable, yet flexible and have the knowledge and experience sought by the protégé. Providing critical, yet constructive feedback is crucial for the mentor to help the protégé grow.[35] Seeking constructive feedback can be a natural outgrowth when an individual must address low performance ratings.[36]

Challenges with Informal Mentoring

However, informal mentoring is not a perfect system, and there are negative aspects. A frequent critique of informal mentoring is that the process may have unclear goals.[37] The challenge resides with the mentor to ensure the purpose is well defined and goals are clear. Additionally, the mentor should engage in discussion of practical scenarios that cannot be addressed through professional development.[38]

While formation of informal relationships is often organic, success is predicated on two self-motivated individuals seeking to form a bond.[39] Fostering an open-door policy and approach is a proactive way that leaders can positively affect the organizational culture and encourage others to engage in informal mentoring.[40] Informal mentors must carefully listen and cultivate trust to develop intense learning that is requisite for leadership preparation.[41]

Because there is no official involvement by organizational leaders, there is minimal control over the process of informal mentoring. Additionally, individuals will seek mentors with whom they are comfortable, not necessarily a mentor who will "push beyond a comfort zone." With no time requirement, there might not be a commitment to overcome any adversity in the relationship, which is necessary if conflict arises between mentor and protégé.[42]

Finally, some researchers argue that a mentor must not be a direct supervisor, or have an evaluative oversight regarding the protégé.[43] However, there is a counterargument that a supervisor can still be an effective mentor *if* there is a high level of trust. The mentoring relationship has to be constructive, and the mentor must display a desire to help the protégé advance in his or her career. Even in a formal setting, there will be informal interactions, as a dichotomy between formal and informal is a tactical dimension of socialization for new leaders.[44]

Benefits of Structured Mentoring Programs	**Benefits of Informal Mentoring Programs**
• High level of control • Effective tool to transmit institutional knowledge • Incentives can be provided • Can serve as a retention initiative • Helps to build and sustain a positive organizational climate	• Sought by the individual because of support • Described positively by mentors and protégés • May develop because of the limitations of structured programs • Convenient for both and flexibility allows for authentic growth
Negatives of Structured Mentoring Programs	**Negatives of Informal Mentoring Programs**
• May not be an emotional connection between mentor and protégé • Hierarchical issues can prevent effective pairings • Financial incentives can be a reason ineffective individuals volunteer	• May have unclear goals • Will only occur if both are motivated individuals • No institutional control over the process • No guarantee of the mentor helping the protégé meet specific needs

Figure 9.1. Positive and Negative Aspects for Different Mentoring Types

CONCLUDING THOUGHTS

Structured and informal opportunities are needed for quality mentoring for effective succession planning. Although a structured program is controlled by senior-level leaders, leadership candidates must be encouraged to seek informal mentors and, in doing so, take responsibility for their own development. The positive and negative highlights are shown in Figure 9.1.

Structured mentoring programs are beneficial because there is a high level of control exercised by leaders in the organization. Great care can be given in matching individuals for myriad reasons. A formal program is one of the most prominent methods for ensuring institutional knowledge is passed to new employees. In general, the process can be used to build and sustain a positive organizational culture.

Informal mentoring is often convenient when an individual simply needs to have an answer quickly. Finding a mentor is often an organic function with trust naturally developing. As long as the mentor and protégé are adaptive and flexible with a growth mind-set, then the process should be beneficial for both. To overcome the inherent problems, the mentor must set clear expectations and goals, provide opportunities that are typically beyond the professional development offerings, and "stretch" assignments provided for the leadership candidate.

Regardless of formal or informal, a mentor must be trustworthy and competent, and typically have greater experience than the protégé. Adaptivity, flexibility, and commitment to a growth mind-set are also common qualities of effective mentors. Being supportive and providing career advice and perspective are often needed by a protégé; however, above all else, for mentoring to be effective, there must be a very high level of trust!

CHAPTER REFERENCES

1. Zepeda, S. J., Bengtson, E., & Parylo, O. (2012). Examining the planning and management of principal succession. *Journal of Educational Administration*, 50(2), 136–158. https://doi.org/10.1108/09578231211210512

2. Collins-Camargo, C., & Kelly, M. J. (2006). Supervisor as informal mentor. *Clinical Supervisor*, 25(1–2), 127–146. https://doi.org/10.1300/j001v25n01_09

Ragins, B. R. (2016). From the ordinary to the extraordinary: High-quality mentoring relationships at work. *Organizational Dynamics*, 45(3), 228–244.

3. Chang, H. (2008). *Autoethnography as method*. Left Coast Press.

4. *ibid.*—Ragins (2016)

ibid.—Zepeda, Bengtson, & Parylo (2012)

5. *ibid.*—Ragins (2016)

6. Ragins, B. R., Cotton, J. L., & Miller, J. S. (2000). Marginal mentoring: The effects of type of mentor, quality of relationship, and program design on work and career attitudes. *Academy of Management Journal, 43*(6), 1177–1194.

7. ibid.—Collins-Camargo & Kelly (2006)

8. Holt, D. T., Markova, G., Dhaenens, A. J., Marler, L. E., & Heilmann, S. G. (2016). Formal or informal mentoring: What drives employees to seek informal mentors? *Journal of Management Issues, 28*(1–2), 67–82.

Kerlin, C. (2016). The mentor inside you. *College and University, 91*(4), 33–36.

9. ibid.—Collins-Camargo & Kelly (2006)

10. Chun, J. U., Sosik, J. J., & Yun, N. Y. (2012). A longitudinal study of mentor and protégé outcomes in formal mentoring relationships. *Journal of Organizational Behavior, 33*(8), 1071–1094.

11. Parfitt, C. M. (2017). Perceptions of succession planning in four Florida school districts: A mixed-method study. *Southeast Journal of Educational Administration, 17*(2), 88–115.

12. ibid.—Holt, Markova, Dhaenens, Marler, & Heilmann (2016)

13. ibid.—Chun, Sosik, & Yun (2006)

14. ibid.—Holt, Markova, Dhaenens, Marler, & Heilmann (2016)

15. Attributed to Dorothy C. Rea, Ph.D., associate professor (retired), Florida Gulf Coast University.

16. Lewis, L. J. (2013). *Capturing tacit knowledge through strategic succession planning: A phenomenological explication* (Publication No. 3557881) [Doctoral dissertation, Baker College]. ProQuest Dissertations and Theses Global.

17. Hopkins-Thompson, P. A. (2000). Colleagues helping colleagues: Mentoring and coaching. *NASSP Bulletin, 84*(617), 29–36.

18. Hengel, R. I. (2007). *Leadership capacity: Planning for leadership succession in schools* (Publication No. 304719536) [Master's thesis, Royal Roads University]. ProQuest Dissertations and Theses Global.

19. Neefe, D. O. (2009). *Succession planning in a two-year technical college system* (Publication No. 3360378) [Doctoral dissertation, University of Minnesota]. ProQuest Dissertations and Theses Global.

20. ibid.—Parfitt (2017)

21. Fullan, M. (2005). *Sustainable leadership*. Corwin Press.

22. Macmillan, R. B., Myers, M. J., & Northfield, S. (2014). Trust and its role in principal succession: A preliminary examination of a continuum of trust. *Leadership and Policy in Schools, 3*(4), 275–294. https://doi.org/10.1080/15700760490901993

23. Santacrose, D. M. (2016). *A mixed-methods study on the perceived role of novice assistant principals and the essence of their lived experience* (Publication No. 10246160) [Doctoral dissertation, Florida Gulf Coast University]. ProQuest Dissertations and Theses Global.

24. ibid.—Collins-Camargo & Kelly (2006)

25. ibid.

26. ibid.—Holt, Markova, Dhaenens, Marler, & Heilmann (2016)
ibid.—Parfitt (2017)

27. ibid.

28. James, J. M., Rayner, A., & Bruno, J. (2015). Are you my mentor? New perspectives and research on informal mentorship. *Journal of Academic Librarianship, 41*(2015), 532–539.

29. *ibid.*—Zepeda, Bengtson, & Parylo (2012)

30. *ibid.*—Ragins (2016)

31. *ibid.*—Holt, Markova, Dhaenens, Marler, & Heilmann (2016)

32. *ibid.*—James, Rayner, & Bruno (2015)

33. Parfitt, C. M., & Rose, A. L. (2020). Informal mentoring for aspiring school leaders: A phenomenological study. *Mentoring and Tutoring: Partnership in Learning, 28*(3), 278–294. https://doi.org/10.1080/13611267.2020.1778837

34. *ibid.*—Collins-Camargo & Kelly (2006)
ibid.—James, Rayner, & Bruno (2015)
ibid.—Ragins (2016)

35. *ibid.*—Parfitt & Rose (2020)

36. *ibid.*—Holt, Markova, Dhaenens, Marler, & Heilmann (2016)

37. Smallwood, C., & Tolley-Stokes, R. (2012). *Mentoring in librarianship: Essays on working with adults and students to further the profession.* McFarland and Company.

38. Lester, P. B., Hannah, S. T., Harms, P. D., Vogelgesang, G. R., & Avolio, B. J. (2011). Mentoring impact on leader efficacy development: A field experiment. *Academy of Management Learning and Education, 10*(3), 409–429.

39. *ibid.*—James, Rayner, & Bruno (2015)

40. *ibid.*—Parfitt & Rose (2020)

41. Browne-Ferrigno, T., & Muth, R. (2004). Leadership mentoring in clinical practice: Role socialization, professional development, and capacity building. *Educational Administration Quarterly, 40*(4), 468–494.

42. *ibid.*—Ragins (2016)

43. *ibid.*—Hopkins-Thompson (2000)

44. Bengtson, E., Zepeda, S. J., & Parylo, O. (2013). School systems practices of controlling socialization during principal succession: Looking through the lens of organization socialization theory. *Educational Management Administration and Leadership, 41*(2), 143–164.

Chapter 10

Issues of Retention

Among scholarly sources, retention is often treated anecdotally; researchers address the importance of retention and may provide some information pertaining to the topic, but most lack empirical evidence. As the third of the major components to proper succession planning, this chapter is focused on the problems with retaining high-performing employees, while the following chapter will have a focus on the practical solutions for retention.

Albeit a simple question, how is retention defined? Depending on one's definition, the answers can change drastically. In the simplest terms, static retention is a consideration that an individual has a particular role and position, and over the analyzed timeframe, the individual remained in the exact same position.[1] But, what if the person accepted a promotion or changed positions and moved laterally? Using a static formula, the individual was not retained.

Are there times when using a static formula is appropriate? Certainly, if it important to document how long individuals remain in specific positions. Having school principals serve an average of 11 years is not necessarily a positive attribute if they are moved from school to school every few years. In most cases, if a principal does not remain in a position for a minimum of four to six years, then no lasting positive changes will be enculturated.[2]

As opposed to a static formula, dynamic retention analysis will usually be a better measure. Using a dynamic measure will permit one to analyze retention within an organization.[3] Over time, knowing that individuals are remaining with the organization, but accepting promotions or moving into different positions, can be quite helpful. Dynamic analysis is also useful in showing trends that might not otherwise be noticed. Do a substantial number of teachers leave a particular school to work at others? Do a noticeable number of individuals become administrators after being teachers in a certain school?

The potential negative for using a dynamic measure is the possibility of skewed data. There may be a high percentage of individuals retained in an organization based on a dynamic measure, but if a static measure yields a low percentage, then there is a high probability of internal issues pertaining to organizational culture. For the most complete analysis, a combination of dynamic and static measures should be used. See Figure 10.1 for an overview of the positive and negative aspects of static and dynamic retention measures.

RIGHT PEOPLE IN THE RIGHT SEATS

In his book on leadership, Jim Collins used an analogy of not only having the right people on the bus but also having those individuals in the right seats.[4]

Benefits of Static Retention Measures	Benefits of Dynamic Retention Measures
• Exact consistency over time • Easiest measure to calculate • Can be used to highlight specific organizational culture problems quickly	• Ability to track interior movement and longevity • Better to document overall organizational stability • Can be used to document promotions and lateral transfers
Negatives of Static Retention Measures	**Negatives of Dynamic Retention Measures**
• Does not account for internal movement • Simplicity does not often convey enough information • Will always produce a lower number than a dynamic report	• May mask internal problems • Greater difficulty in tracking movement • Greater time and resources needed to ensure accurate data

Figure 10.1. Aspects for Static and Dynamic Retention Measures

Regardless of whether a dynamic or static measure is used, a pure quantitative measure will not yield enough actionable information. For example, a school with 26% turnover quantitatively would be viewed as less effective than a school with 10% turnover. However, if the first school had seven of the lowest performing teachers leave because they were not meeting stringent expectations compared to three of the highest performing teachers leave school two because of poor climate, which was really worse?

The most important question to ask is *"why?"* The focus is mitigation, because individuals "will continue to retire, leave the organization, or change to new jobs."[5] The key in understanding why is to prevent unnecessary losses to the maximum extent possible. However, it is important to note that a robust and effective succession-planning process will increase the probability that some well-trained and prepared employees will seek promotional opportunities with other organizations.[6]

Having a pool with many qualified individuals prepared to assume positions of greater authority knowing that some will seek other opportunities is vastly preferred to having few individuals ready or vacancies for which there is no individual prepared.[7] From a leadership standpoint, beyond the responsibility to train future leaders as a requisite job function, some equate it as a moral responsibility to the profession.[8]

COST VERSUS "COST"

Preparing future leaders certainly has a cost, but which is greater: replacing a stellar employee or retaining a stellar employee? Direct and indirect replacement costs were briefly mentioned in Chapter 7 with poorly handled processes costing in excess of 200% of the position salary.[9] In addition to the financial return on investment, retaining an internal candidate means the employee already has demonstrated some level of competence and knows the organizational culture.[10]

Even by calculating indirect costs, the true measure of losing an exemplary leader with no one prepared to assume the position cannot be determined. "The pain felt watching a star employee walk out the door with no backup in place is immediate and costly." Naturally, the costs increase at administrative and executive levels.[11] Unfortunately, such losses are usually avoidable to a certain extent; failure to deliver on promises of upward mobility and a lack of input are prime reasons individuals give for leaving an organization.[12]

GAMBLING WITH THE NUMBERS

Unfortunately, large-scale survey results for succession planning in education are not generally available; considering the fact that business enterprises have recognized the importance of quality succession planning for decades, the number of Fortune 500 companies without comprehensive plans within the last decade is almost shocking.[13] Using the assertion that education as a discipline is typically lacking in implementing best practices developed in other fields, one can surmise that educational entities have an even greater gap with succession planning.[14]

From a 2015 review of perceptions of approximately 1,100 business executives, only 8% of the respondents indicated that an individual in the organization was prepared to assume an executive position immediately, while another 27% stated that someone could assume an executive-level position but would require intensive training to meet basic requirements. However, almost two out of three Fortune 500 companies were not prepared for an unexpected departure of executive-level employees at all.[15]

Although quality succession planning should be used to address positions at all levels of the organization, many of the companies with plans do not sufficiently have initiatives for middle- and lower-level positions. From the same 2015 review, only 9% of respondents indicated a succession plan was in place and internal candidates were prepared to assume middle-management positions. Additionally, only 14% of the respondents indicated that internal candidates were prepared to assume lower-level management positions.[16]

While the purpose of a quality succession plan is to have a pool of qualified individuals prepared to assume positions of greater responsibility at all levels with a forward-thinking assumption, a quality plan is also important to overcome tragic and unexpected losses. From a business standpoint, those companies with a defined plan fared better through tragic losses of a CEO than did those without a plan.[17] Those companies without a plan experienced a plummet in stock price and diminished cash flow.[18]

While surviving a terrible loss should not be the primary reason to have a quality succession plan, the disequilibrium and uncertainty caused by executive turnover increases the likelihood of employees leaving. This is a reason why some of the earliest studies pertaining to succession planning focused on the organizational instability following a change in CEO.[19] A trend that was noted around the turn of the last century in those situations was to promote individuals early as a retention effort and keep those promising individuals from seeking other opportunities.[20]

FAILURE TO REWARD

A linkage between reward systems and retention is often cited by authors in various disciplines,[21] yet minimal empirical evidence has been produced to show the positive effects; most researchers have focused on the antithesis, and the negative results from poor retention efforts, or relied on anecdotal evidence to show the importance of retention. The assertion is naturally logical, though, because salary and benefits are almost always among the reasons cited for educators leaving the profession.[22]

An aspect that had not been considered much by researchers is the effect when rewards are only considered for top-level positions. Promoting a promising individual to chief operating officer was a strategy often used in Fortune 500 companies to keep a stellar individual, but when an individual was then promoted to CEO, 83% of the companies had not filled the chief operating officer position by the next fiscal year.[23]

Although the focus was recognized by the 1990s, a quality plan must be written to address all levels of the organization.[24] The fact a number two position for a Fortune 500 company could remain vacant for a year is itself evidence of a lack of planning for subordinate levels. The same is often true for school districts; most school boards will be diligent in ensuring an acting or interim superintendent is in place, but deputy or associate superintendent positions may remain unfilled for several months or longer.

The same argument can be made for school-based positions. The role of assistant principal can be ambiguous or ill defined.[25] Albeit mostly qualitative studies pertaining to the viewpoints of individuals serving as assistant principal reflect that the individuals often view uncertainty in expectations and, depending upon the leadership style of the principal, do not have many opportunities to exercise leadership appropriately.[26]

The old adage about the most difficult job as a musician is second violin is very similar to subordinate leadership positions in educational entities. Stellar assistant principals often view part of their role is "to make the boss look good," even knowing that minimal, if any, credit is ever given.[27] Unfortunately, when no credit is given and minimal appreciation is shown, a promising leadership candidate has a far greater likelihood of leaving the organization. Money and prestige are not the top motivators; lack of appreciation and support is the primary reason for departure at all levels in education.[28]

ADDRESSING ASPIRATIONS

Beyond appreciation and support, many business and psychology authors have suggested to have annual discussions with employees about their future plans and aspirations.[29] As William Rothwell contended, preparing individuals for positions of greater authority should be viewed in terms of two promotions.[30] Unfortunately, a futuristic plan has often been lacking in education, but so have conversations and discussions. In many instances, current school leaders are not aware of the aspirations of some employees, and informal encouragement is generally the extent of feedback from current principals.[31]

Knowing which individuals have aspirations for greater positions, and which do not, is certainly helpful in planning and for ensuring rewards are commensurate to keep high-performing talent. For instance, a greater number of secondary assistant principals are content in remaining as assistant principals compared to those in primary schools. Some individuals aspire to have a central-office position, but not all wish to become superintendent, and some wish to remain in lower positions. Having the information helps plan accordingly.[32]

Autonomy on writing goals is a minor contributing factor to the lack of discussion for employee aspirations.[33] Too often, individuals are not able to write true professional goals; there must be specific aspects or categories addressed and some type of caveat or mandate addressed. Instead of having a discussion pertaining to professional growth, the planning meetings for goals often end up centering on rewriting a performance goal to show that 80% of students have demonstrated proficiency on a standardized test . . .

UNWILLINGNESS TO ADDRESS THE ROOT CAUSES

Asking employees about their aspirations is important, but presumably few individuals are leaving an educational organization because a futuristic conversation did not occur. Unfortunately, one of the greatest problems is only shown through a secondary approach. Lack of administrative support is the most frequently cited issue;[34] however, lack of support is from the viewpoint of the subordinate. If lack of support has been identified as a prime reason for 20 years, then what has been done to address the concern? Unfortunately, almost nothing.

The problem stems from the highest levels downward. A central-office administrator was questioned by school board members as to why two similar schools had drastically different outcomes. Although the schools were geographically only one mile apart situated on the same main road, one school was thriving and successful, while the other school was plagued with high teacher turnover, low student enrollment, and a poor reputation.

The board members questioned whether the schools were located in drastically different neighborhoods, had a widely differing population of students, were equipped with different facilities, or demonstrated any other possible variance. When the administrator mentioned that the first school had a dynamic and collaborative principal while the second had a micromanaging, authoritarian principal, the board members immediately ended discussion; they did not want to listen to the root cause.

Both schools should have had equal success, but poor leadership precluded the second from achieving success. Far too often, ineffective and utterly incompetent individuals are left in leadership positions; yet the ramifications are rarely discussed. For the second school, low morale and high turnover were a result. Once a school has developed a negative reputation, there is a far greater difficulty in overcoming the challenges. Poor-performing schools are then often staffed with the least prepared teachers.[35] A negative and self-fulfilling trend is then established.

CONCLUDING THOUGHTS

As was mentioned at the beginning of the chapter, retention in scholarly literature is often treated anecdotally. But, without large-scale educational studies, anecdotal and qualitative information is the basis from which one must make assumptions. Considering that education as a discipline is often several years behind other fields, business leaders have recognized the importance of quality succession planning for more than 30 years, and nearly two-thirds of Fortune 500 businesses do not have comprehensive plans, then one can surmise that educational entities are in "worse shape."

A combination of static and dynamic measures is truly needed to document retention effectively. Specific benchmarks were not provided for a reason, as each organization is going to be different and the culture will be different. In one setting, 5% turnover could be considered terrible, and in another 20% could be considered a tremendous success. Of importance, for a school-based setting, if a principal does not spend four to six years in a position, the chances of lasting change will be minimal. Establishment of positive culture takes time, and overcoming negative aspects takes even longer.

Failing to provide rewards and incentives, lack of futuristic engagement, and an unwillingness to address problems are all major contributing factors to a lack of retention. Providing appropriate support must be the first and foremost task of a leader. Replacing a stellar employee is far costlier than retaining a stellar employee. The indirect costs alone should provide enough of a rationale for focusing on retention.

CHAPTER REFERENCES

1. Farley-Ripple, E. N., Solano, P. L., & McDuffie, M. J. (2012). Conceptual and methodological issues in research on school administrator career behavior. *Educational Researcher, 41*(6), 220–229. https://doi.org/10.3102/0013189X12451774

2. Hargreaves, A. (2005). Leadership succession. *Educational Forum, 69*(2), 163–173. https://doi.org/10.1080/00131720508984680

Zepeda, S. J., Bengtson, E., & Parylo, O. (2012). Examining the planning and management of principal succession. *Journal of Educational Administration, 50*(2), 136–158. https://doi.org/10.1108/09578231211210512

3. *ibid.*—Farley-Ripple, Solano, & McDuffie (2012)

4. Collins, J. (2001). *Good to great: Why some companies make the leap and others don't.* Harper Business.

5. Spradling, S. (2021). *Transformational leadership in education: The impact of succession planning for the nursing professional development specialist* [Unpublished doctoral dissertation]. American Sentinel College of Nursing.

6. Smeltzer, C. H. (2002). Succession planning. *Journal of Nursing Administration, 32*(12), 615.

7. *ibid.*

8. *ibid.*

9. Allen, D. G. (2006). *Retaining talent: A guide to analyzing and managing employee turnover* (SHRM Foundation's effective practice guidelines series). Society for Human Resources Management.

10. Chavez, J. (2011). The case for succession planning. *Strategic Finance, 92*(8), 15–16.

11. McDonald, P. (2015, August 27). *Few employees waiting in the wings: Survey suggests succession plans lacking at all levels.* Robert Half Management Resources. http://www.prnewswire.com/news-releases/few-employeeswaiting-in-the-wings-survey-suggests-succession-plans-lacking-at-all-levels-300133964.html

12. Cappelli, P., & Hamori, M. (2004). *The path to the top: Changes in the attributes of corporate executives, 1980–2001* (Working Paper 10507). National Bureau of Economic Research. https://doi.org/10.3386/w10507

13. *ibid.*—McDonald (2015)

14. Riddick, F. P. (2009). *What is your bench strength? An exploration of succession planning in three large school districts in a southeastern state* (Publication No. 3360378) [Doctoral dissertation, North Carolina State University]. ProQuest Dissertations and Theses Global.

15. *ibid.*—McDonald (2015)

16. *ibid.*

17. Gurchiek, K. (2015, November 15). *Don't leave succession planning to chance.* Society for Human Resource Management. https://www.shrm.org/hrdisciplines/

orgempdev/articles/pages/leadership-manyorganizations-fail-at-succession-planning.aspx

18. Behn, B. K., Riley, R. A., Jr., & Yang, Y. (2005). The value of an heir apparent in succession planning. *Corporate Governance, 13*(2), 168–177.

19. Grusky, O. (1960). Administrative succession in formal organizations. *Social Forces, 39*(2), 105–115.

20. Beeson, J. (2000). Succession planning: Leading-edge practices: What the best companies are doing. *Across the Board, 37*(2), 38–41.

21. Beeson, J. (1998). Succession planning: Building the management corps. *Business Horizons, 41*(5), 61–66.

Griffith, M. B. (2012). Effective succession planning in nursing: A review of the literature. *Journal of Nursing Management, 20*(7), 900–911. https://doi.org/10.1111/j.1365-2834.2012.01418.x

22. Chase, B. (2000). Show us the money. *NEA Today, 18*(7), 5.

Darling-Hammond, L. (2001). The challenge of staffing our schools. *Educational Leadership, 58*(8), 12–17.

Ingersoll, R. M. (2001). Teacher turnover and teacher shortages: An organizational analysis. *American Educational Research Journal, 38*(3), 499–534.

Newberry, M., & Alsopp, Y. (2017). Teacher attrition in the USA: The relational elements in a Utah case study. *Teachers and Teaching: Theory and Practice, 23*(8), 863–880. https://doi.org/10.1080/13540602.2017.1358705

23. Bennett, N., & Miles, S. A. (2006, May). Second in command: The misunderstood role of the chief operating officer. *Harvard Business Review*, 71–78.

24. *ibid.*—Beeson (1998)

25. Hausman, C., Nebeker, A., McCreary, J., & Donaldson, G. (2002). The worklife of the assistant principal. *Journal of Educational Administration, 40*(2/3), 136–157. https://doi.org/10.1108/09578230210421105

26. Karpinski, C. F. (2008). "This is my school, not yours": A novice assistant principal's attempt to lead. *Journal of Cases in Educational Leadership, 11*(1), 87–96. https://doi.org/10.1177/1555458908326614

27. Parfitt, C. M., Romano, B. M., Hudzina, D. M., & Rogozinski, S. G. (2020). Perceptions of leadership identification: A collective autoethnographical study. *Voices of Reform: Educational Research to Inform and Reform, 3*(2), 82–95. https://doi.org/10.32623/3.10006

28. *ibid.*—Chase (2000)
ibid.—Darling-Hammond (2001)
ibid.—Ingersoll (2001)
ibid.—Newberry & Alsopp (2017)

29. De Clercq, D. (2021). Getting nowhere, going elsewhere: The impact of perceived career compromises on turnover intentions. *Personnel Review*. Advance Online Publication. https://doi.org/10.1108/PR-08-2020-0603

Pandey, M. K., & Tripathi, P. (2018). Examine the relationship between level of aspiration, believes in just world, psychological well-being and quality of work-life. *Indian Journal of Health and Wellbeing, 9*(1), 53–59.

30. Rothwell, W. J. (2005). *Effective succession planning: Ensuring leadership continuity and building talent from within* (3rd ed.). AMACOM.

31. *ibid.*—Parfitt, Romano, Hudzina, & Rogozinski (2020)

32. Croft, J. C., & Morton, J. R. (1977, April 5–8). *The assistant principal: In quandry or comfort? [Paper presentation].* American Educational Research Association Annual Meeting, New York, NY (ED136392). ERIC. https://files.eric.ed.gov/fulltext/ED136392.pdf

Pellicer, L. O., & Stevenson, K. R. (1991). The assistant principalship as a legitimate terminal career alternative. *NASSP Bulletin, 75*(533), 59–65. https://doi.org/10.1177/019263659107553312

33. Reisinger, H., & Fetterer, D. (2021, October 29). Forget flexibility; Your employees want autonomy. *Harvard Business Review.* https://hbr.org/2021/10/forget-flexibility-your-employees-want-autonomy

34. *ibid.*—Chase (2000)

ibid.—Darling-Hammond (2001)

ibid.—Ingersoll (2001)

ibid.—Newberry & Alsopp (2017)

35. Lewis-Spector, J. (2016). State-level regulations for alternative routes to teacher certification in the U.S.: Are candidates being prepared to develop their students' literacy? *Literacy Practice and Research, 42*(1), 5–15.

Chapter 11

Practical Solutions for Retention

One aspect should hopefully be clear from the prior chapter: unlike other facets of succession planning, retention has the most variability and the least predictability because of myriad factors involved. Unfortunately, all of the best practices can be identified and implemented, and careful consideration of the organizational culture can be taken in every regard, yet a stellar leader will leave the organization. Spouses are transferred across the country because of a job, someone may need to care for an elderly or infirm family member; all of those facets and numerous others cannot be addressed through retention efforts.

Among the most frequently cited reasons educators leave the profession, some of the underlying reasons cannot be changed: physical location of facilities, the working hours required because of the transportation systems, and, to an extent, within reason even salaries. The most substantially cited reason is usually lack of support,[1] which is unfortunate because support is one component over which there is considerable control.

PROVIDING ADMINISTRATIVE SUPPORT

Providing appropriate support must be among the foremost responsibilities of senior leaders, and to ensure mid-level leaders are also providing support to their subordinates.[2] To aid in the discussion, Case Study 11.1 (see Figure 11.1) contains a fictional account of individuals enrolled in a district-based principal preparation program, and the reader is to view the challenges as the director of human resources would. Throughout the chapter, additional information will be provided to help make a determination about securing appropriate measures to ensure the individuals remain with the school district.

With any case study, only a limited amount of information can be provided, and therefore the reader must make certain assumptions. However, the assumptions are critical in addressing the potential concerns of the

Case Study 11.1

Determining a Flight Risk

Congratulations, you have been promoted to director of human resources for North Canyon School District, which primarily serves an urban center with some surrounding areas. You report directly to the superintendent as the member of the cabinet and have a one-on-one meeting every Monday. Fortunately, your predecessor had a concern for leadership development and there is a formal program with components at varying stages of readiness.

At your most recent meeting, the superintendent was concerned because there have been "murmurings through the grapevine" that a substantial number of administrative personnel have been discussing seeking opportunities elsewhere. Supposedly, many are unhappy with recent central-office personnel changes and principal appointments. The school board had recently approved expanding the budget for leadership development, and the superintendent believes that the board members will view high-profile departures very negatively.

A principal preparation cohort started by your predecessor is nearing completion. Because those individuals represent a suitable cross-section of school district personnel, determining their likelihood of leaving would be an appropriate first step to make recommendations for retention initiatives.

Throughout the chapter, additional information will be provided for the five fictional individuals listed in Case Study 11.1. Your job as director of human resources is to determine the extent each is a risk of leaving and what measures could potentially be used to entice each to stay.

Jennifer Penelope has been assistant principal of Northern Elementary School for 6 years and was a teacher for 16 years before. She intentionally bought a house to live near the school. Her current principal is known to be a good mentor whom she trusts, and he has relayed that Jennifer has remained a loyal employee despite having experienced a terribly abusive situation in the past. One potential negative aspect is that Mrs. Penelope has been vocal about administrator pay compared to other local school districts. She has two children who attend schools in the district including a child with special needs.

David Skye is the assistant principal of curriculum for Four Mile River Middle School, having been transferred into the position this year. Previously, he served as assistant principal for 4 years at Junction Elementary School. David is considered to be impatient and marginally arrogant. He expects to be in a senior

> leadership position in a few years. Mr. Skye has been clear that he is willing to move to ensure he has the proper experiences to succeed in the future, and he will not remain in a setting if appropriate opportunities are not offered.
>
> Michelle Williams is considered to be a fast-track success story. She completed her first college degree at a young age, was accepted into a leadership program as soon as she had the minimum required experience, and is currently enrolled in a doctoral program. She became assistant principal at Ocean View High School during her 5th year teaching. Michelle just turned 30 and will meet the requirements to be considered to be principal upon completion of the current academic year. Ms. Williams has been known to speak about the importance of quality of life, but also being in the proper setting and treated appropriately.
>
> Brian Jacobs has been assistant principal of Eagle Middle School for 4 years, and was a teacher at Panther Middle School for 11 years. He knows the community well, having two older brothers and father who are school administrators. Although considered an exceptional leader, Brian is always comparing himself to his brothers. He expects to "make a name for himself," but he also has made comments about needing to "step out of the shadows" of his family members.
>
> James Lorenzo is a model employee. He has been assistant principal of Rivergate Elementary School for 9 years, and was a teacher in the district for 10 prior years. Mr. Lorenzo holds an additional master's degree in reading education. Always known for seeking the best for his students, James's reputation is that others have sought his expertise, and he has been approached by educational technology companies previously.

Figure 11.1. Determining a Flight Risk

individuals. "Throwing money at the problem," may not be a realistic nor appropriate solution at all.[3] Deciphering what steps can be taken is not an easy task, but taking no action often has far worse consequences.

DIAGNOSING A PROBLEM

Albeit cliché, the first step in addressing a problem is admitting the problem exists. As mentioned in Chapter 7, one of the duties of human-resources officials is to provide warnings to senior leaders about the dangers from a lack of quality succession planning.[4] Fortunately, from the information provided in Case Study 11.1, the superintendent of the school district is already aware of the problem and will be supportive of corrective action. In a situation, if the requisite leaders are not aware, then the first responsibility is to raise awareness of the problem. Then, create an appropriate remedy and secure support.

Examining the fictional characters from the case study will provide some important points on which to focus. For example, the first character, Mrs. Penelope, does not seem to be a high risk of leaving immediately; she was mistreated by a previous supervisor, has children who are involved in special programs, and lives near her place of employment. However, she clearly indicated pay as a concern. While pay is not foremost among reasons educators leave, pay is usually among the top 10 reasons.[5] At what point does the pay gap become enough of a reason?

The second character, Mr. Skye, has fewer reasons to stay. However, just because he is impatient does not guarantee he is ready for greater responsibility. As a rising star, Ms. Williams is presumably the type of employee who should be a prime focus to retain. From the information provided, she appears to be pleased at the moment but is unclear whether she would leave for a better opportunity.

The fourth character, Mr. Jacobs, has mixed reasons to stay. Community and family ties are important, but when considering the statements about "making a name for himself," he could be a "flight risk." Mr. Lorenzo, the fifth character, is most likely not at risk of leaving for another position in a primary or secondary school but most likely to accept a corporate position. So, given the information at hand, there is not enough information to ensure these fictional characters will remain in the school district. Interviewing directly may be a possibility, but if they are truly seeking other employment, would they tell?

ALWAYS A LEARNING CURVE

While frequently conducting a climate study using a validated instrument would provide beneficial information,[6] the cost and time would be prohibitive. Just as knowing his or her students is important for a teacher, knowing his or her subordinates is important for any leader. "Keeping a finger on the pulse," "keeping an ear to the ground," or any of the other colloquial expressions for assessing organizational culture and climate are apropos.

Every organizational culture will be different, and no two organizations will be alike, so there is no universal system to monitor. However, there are concepts worth exploring. "Management by Walking Around" was a concept that originated in the 1940s by David Packard, and its premise is relatively straightforward: engage with employees directly in their own environments.

With the proliferation of online meetings, the concept can be enacted digitally to interact with employees.[7]

In essence, creating a positive organizational culture is the most practical solution for increasing employee retention. In a people-driven enterprise such as education, managing the talent within the organization effectively is a route to positive culture. Unfortunately, there have been few academic studies in which the connection has been researched. However, some work has been completed through resource-based view theory and social exchange theory approaches in which the connection between talent management and retention have been posited.[8]

CREATING AND MAINTAINING THE CULTURE

While the importance of culture will be examined in greater detail in Chapter 12, the importance must be noted. Although the focus of her study was attracting students rather than retaining employees, Mahsa Alizadeh contended that when a person is satisfied with an institutional experience, then the likelihood of positive word-of-mouth feedback is increased.[9] Satisfied and engaged employees have a far greater liklihood to bring others to the institution, which would then have a positive effect on retention.

But how does one create a positive culture in which the employees are engaged and satisfied? Simply implementing a strategy or program is not enough to create a positive culture and retain employees. Individuals will always seek better and lucrative opportunities, and nothing can be done to stop their job searches. In fact, as shown in recent data, more than 40% of the American workforce were actively seeking new employment. Among those seeking new opportunities, 56% indicated their direct supervisor was the primary reason for searching.[10]

Therefore, part of the solution is to increase employee loyalty. The culture must be created to address career aspirations and, in doing so, allow for autonomy, authority to delegate appropriately, and the ability to foster collaborative and cooperative arrangements.[11] In addition to the issue of compensation, work and life imbalance was a prime reason cited by 42% of those seeking new employment. More than one-third were seeking better fringe benefits, and one-third simply desired to make a career change because of a lack of job satisfaction.[12]

CONNECTING BACKWARDS

Talent management has been referenced repeatedly and for good reason. Back in Chapter 6, the concept was described as the "heart" of succession planning with trust being the "heartbeat" as described in Chapter 9.[13] Succession planning is a recursive process, and as an example, a very practical solution to foster greater retention is to provide targeted and specific development opportunities to employees.

Several researchers from Prairie View A&M University provided a training and development framework to add in retention. The two simultaneous prongs are increased job content and responsibilities, and increased formal training and development.[14] In essence, a quality succession plan contains phases for specific and targeted development and mentoring, which are needed to ensure a continuous pipeline of candidates prepared to assume positions of greater responsibility, but the same actions add in retaining high-performing employees.

The increasing job content and responsibilities prong includes (a) increased autonomy to make decisions, (b) opportunities to determine goals and priorities, (c) increased supervisory assignments, (d) greater interactions with superordinates, and (e) cross-training opportunities.[15] One important note: increased opportunities and responsibilities are need for employees at all levels, not just those who aspiring for career advancement.

The increased formal training and development prong includes activities such as (a) assisting with tuition for additional formal education, (b) funding for external seminars and conferences, (c) offering opportunities for virtual trainings, (d) providing commonly needed trainings frequently, and (e) allowing for training and development in areas of interest of the employee, not just predetermined categories aligned to strategic directions.[16]

A RETURN TO ASSESSMENT

Just as appropriate assessment was needed for identification of talent, then development strategies, it is also needed for retention efforts. Appropriate performance appraisal is bidirectional, meaning the employee receives targeted feedback on strengths and weaknesses, and data are provided to senior leaders pertaining to organizational performance, as well as the employee-to-supervisor relationship.[17]

One important aspect is that assessment for retention must contain a solicitation of feedback *from* the employee, not just *about* the employee, because not all feedback is valid.[18] What are the perceptions of employees?

Are teachers leaving one school to join another, or are they leaving the school district completely? Do support staff members seem appreciated and valued? Are appropriate opportunities and challenges being presented? Those factors among many others need to be considered and analyzed.

Returning to the point of a comprehensive climate study being valuable yet often cost and time prohibitive: as long as senior leaders are using strategies to "keep a finger on the pulse," or "know what is going on" today, then information can be collected anecdotally and informally. One does not need a formal climate study in which the mean score of 1.7 for an item pertaining to positive work environment to know there are cultural issues. "Hearing through the grapevine" that 14 teachers are requesting a transfer from Mount Rushmore Middle School is enough information to know corrective action is needed to address the culture.

ADDRESSING THE CASES

While the practical solutions and recommendations presented in this chapter are only a fraction of possibilities, and most are vague and lack certain specificity, the answer is always because the unique and specific organizational culture will be different in every organization. But with an incomplete assessment and the limited information provided, recommendations can be made to address the concerns for the flight risk of the fictional characters.

There are several factors to address. The information in the case study is incomplete. What mistreatment did Mrs. Penelope receive from a previous supervisor and when? How was the situation resolved, and what steps were taken to avoid a repeat occurrence? Major "red flags" for organizational culture need to be addressed. If 42% are already seeking new employment, and 56% of those cite a current supervisor as a reason,[19] then logically nearly one-quarter of all employees are seeking new opportunities because of a supervisor. Do not give them additional reasons, and eliminate the issues causing them to leave.

Mr. Skye wants opportunities, which clearly can be addressed by the job content and responsibilities prong of the Prairie View A&M model. Is providing additional opportunities enough of a reason for him to stay? Maybe yes, maybe no. But if nothing is done, what are the reasons for staying? It's the same with Ms. Williams; happiness can be fleeting, and without some reasons provided to stay, would she be inclined to accept a position elsewhere, especially if the pay is substantially greater?

Addressing Mr. Jacobs's concerns are going to be more difficult than the others, because so many of his concerns are connected to intrinsic factors. However, does that mean one should ignore those types of concerns?

Definitely no. What assessments are conducted, and what data are being collected and analyzed? The same is true for Mr. Lorenzo; stopping a person from changing careers might not be a worthwhile challenge, but knowing the reasons and rationale would be very helpful, and only by assessing appropriately will one know.

CONCLUDING THOUGHTS

Compared to many of the previous chapters, an analysis of practical solutions to retention has shown the extent to which quality succession planning is a recursive process, as well as the extent to which culture greatly matters. Leaders at all levels have a crucial function in providing appropriate administrative support and working to create *and* maintain a positive organizational culture and climate.[20]

Regardless of the current state of an organization, leaders must be willing to admit problems exist then take corrective action to address concerns. Having a "finger on the pulse" is essential, and whether achieved by "management by walking around" or some other process, constant assessment of the situation is needed. Only by knowing the thoughts and concerns of individuals will senior leaders be able to plan appropriately.

Finally, providing the appropriate development and training opportunities is a vital facet to establishing a positive organizational culture and engaging employees. Knowing that a great percentage are already seeking opportunities elsewhere, the answer is to provide reasons to stay. Organizational culture matters greatly, and the topic will be addressed in greater detail in the next chapter.

CHAPTER REFERENCES

1. Chase, B. (2000). Show us the money. *NEA Today, 18*(7), 5.

Darling-Hammond, L. (2001). The challenge of staffing our schools. *Educational Leadership, 58*(8), 12–17.

Ingersoll, R. M. (2001). Teacher turnover and teacher shortages: An organizational analysis. *American Educational Research Journal, 38*(3), 499–534.

Newberry, M., & Alsopp, Y. (2017). Teacher attrition in the USA: The relational elements in a Utah case study. *Teachers and Teaching: Theory and Practice, 23*(8), 863–880. https://doi.org/10.1080/13540602.2017.1358705

2. Parfitt, C. M., & Romano, B. M. (2022). Assessing succession-planning processes: A case study for improvement. In L. L. Sabina (Ed.), *School administrator*

succession planning: Identifying high-impact practices, programs, and frameworks in P–12 schools (pp. 187–206). Information Age Publishing.

3. Grissom, J. A., & Bartanen, B. (2019). Principal effectiveness and principal turnover. *Education Finance and Policy*, *14*(3), 355–382. https://doi.org/10.1162/edfp_a_00256

4. Gurchiek, K. (2015, November 15). *Don't leave succession planning to chance*. Society for Human Resource Management. https://www.shrm.org/hrdisciplines/orgempdev/articles/pages/leadership-manyorganizations-fail-at-succession-planning.aspx

5. *ibid.*—Chase (2000)
ibid.—Darling-Hammond (2001)
ibid.—Ingersoll (2001)
ibid.—Newberry & Alsopp (2017)

6. Owens, R. G., & Valesky, T. C. (2022). *Organizational behavior in education: Leadership and school reform* (12th ed.). Pearson Education.

7. McKendrick, J. (2020, April 6). Is "management by walking around"' still possible when everything is digital and remote? *Forbes*. https://www.forbes.com/sites/joemckendrick/2020/04/06/is-management-by-walking-around-still-possible-when-everything-is-digital-and-remote/?sh=1f9033cb4498

8. Narayanan, A., & Manoj Menon, S. R. (2019). Talent management and employee retention: An integrative research framework. *Human Resource Development Review*, *18*(2), 228–247. https://doi.org/10.1177/1534484318812159

9. Alizadeh, M. (2014). *Influential factors in international students' college choice of a rural, regional university* [Doctoral dissertation, Eastern Kentucky University]. Eastern Kentucky University Encompass Online Dissertations and Theses. https://encompass.eku.edu/etd/240

10. Maurer, R., & Mirza, B. (2021, September 12). *Deconstructing the great resignation: SHRM research reveals which employees are leaving and why*. Society for Human Resources Management. https://www.shrm.org/hr-today/news/hr-news/pages/deconstructing-the-great-resignation.aspx

11. Khalid, K., & Nawab, S. (2018). Employee participation and employee retention in view of compensation. *Sage Open*, *8*(4), 1–17. https://doi.org/10.1177/2158244018810067

12. *ibid.*—Maurer & Mirza (2021)

13. Ragins, B. R. (2016). From the ordinary to the extraordinary: High-quality mentoring relationships at work. *Organizational Dynamics*, *45*(3), 228–244.

Zepeda, S. J., Bengtson, E., & Parylo, O. (2012). Examining the planning and management of principal succession. *Journal of Educational Administration*, *50*(2), 136–158. https://doi.org/10.1108/09578231211210

14. Cloutier, O., Felusiak, L., Hill, C., & Pemberton-Jones, E. J. (2015). The importance of developing strategies for employee retention. *Journal of Leadership, Accountability and Ethics*, *12*(2), 119–129.

15. *ibid.*
16. *ibid.*

17. Singh, D. (2019). A literature review on employee retention with focus on recent trends. *International Journal of Science Research in Science Technology*, 6(1), 425–431. https://doi.org/10.32628/IJSRST195463

18. Buckingham, M., & Goodall, A. (2019, March–April). The feedback fallacy. *Harvard Business Review*, 92–101. https://hbr.org/2019/03/the-feedback-fallacy

19. *ibid.*—Maurer & Mirza (2021)

20. *ibid.*—Owens & Valesky (2022)

Chapter 12

The Importance of Culture for Retaining the Best

Organizational culture has been the overarching theme for each chapter, and although this chapter has a focus on culture for retention purposes, and as demonstrated in the previous chapter, the importance of culture throughout each phase and overarching for the process cannot be overstated. In the very first chapter, organizational culture was described as the closest to a panacea and the "silver bullet" for success. The saying was apropos because organizational culture truly is the differentiator for success.

Many great leaders have been ascribed as being the right person, in the right time, in the right place. But success is more than being "lucky" at the correct time. The culture mattered, and the most effective leaders were able to leverage the situation because their charisma, dedication, or brilliance was amplified through the organizational culture. History is replete with examples of those who overcame substantial odds; of course, a vast number of those remembered were political or military leaders. Although the recognition may not be as great, business, civic, religious, and other leaders have had an impact.

George Washington, Alexander the Great, Julius Caesar, Winston Churchill, Mahatma Gandhi, Saint John Paul II, Martin Luther King Jr., Lao Tzu, Abraham Lincoln, George S. Patton, Margaret Thatcher, among so many others were successful because they were deemed the right leader at the right time. Despite any post facto discussion of their flaws, using the previously mentioned work by Morgan McCall, those individuals had the "right stuff," in addition to being in the right setting.[1] In some cases, "one must answer the call when asked to step up to the plate."[2]

NORMS, VALUES, AND BELIEFS

Although the definition was provided in Chapter 1, to ensure consistency, a reiteration of the definition of organizational culture is apropos. As defined by Robert Owens and Thomas Valesky, organizational culture is one of the four components of organizational climate and is primarily composed of the norms, values, and beliefs held by individuals in the organization. There are, of course, other components that fit into the definition of organizational culture.[3]

Understanding the organizational culture is important for employees, potential employees, and especially leaders in the organization. Because in many ways, culture is like glass—very difficult and time consuming to create, but can be shattered beyond repair in a singular moment. Changes in culture are also very time consuming and difficult, and negative aspects are far easier to enculturate than positive change.[4]

POTENTIAL OPTIONS FOR CHANGE

While there are three potential options, only two are valid for effective succession planning. The choice of a laissez-faire approach or simply to "do nothing," is not viable long term for effective succession planning. Therefore, the true options are maintaining a positive organizational culture, or working to build a positive organizational culture. Destruction or reducing positivity in organizational culture could only be done with ill intentions.

A laissez-faire approach *could* be used short term, and thus is included as an option. However, no planning is needed to "do nothing," so there is nothing to contribute to describing a laissez-faire approach. In the same vein as laissez-faire is a desire to avoid conflict. Healthy conflict is positive and can be a catalyst to help move the organization forward; however, destructive conflict is detrimental, and a desire to avoid conflict by leaders is never the answer. Failure to address destructive conflict only causes the underlying problems to become worse.[5]

Maintaining a positive culture is the easier approach; however, it still requires effort and vigilance. Negative aspects can easily be established, and once established perpetuated. As was mentioned in Chapter 11, education is a people-driven enterprise, and it is therefore incumbent on leaders to show value for the employees. Providing opportunities to give input and recommendations and make suggestions are components of productive organizational environment.[6]

Building a positive culture in an organization is one of the prime responsibilities of a leader. The great difficulty is not just creating positive change, but creating lasting positive change. As was mentioned in Chapter 1, sustainability is the needed approach.[7] While sustainability is part of the goal, the process to achieve the goal is to enculturate positive aspects. Forceful and top-down strategies rarely work and usually result in entrenched resistance.[8] To show the importance of quality succession planning encompassing all levels of an organization, positive enculturation and sustainability is achieved through distributed leadership.[9]

No matter how brilliant or exceptional a leader's vision is, without appropriate buy-in from others, nothing else matters. If individuals have been supervised by an authoritarian "leader" for a substantial period of time, suddenly asking them to make decisions and to give flexibility and autonomy may be received with suspicion. Implementing positive change takes time, and using the Japanese principle of *kaizen*—change through small, incremental steps—is most likely appropriate if the culture needs improvement.[10]

While an analogy for building a positive culture can be described as climbing a mountain, maintaining the culture is not the same as simply "having arrived at a destination." Effort is needed to maintain, just as a person in great physical shape must continually exercise. For example, noted jazz saxophonist John Coltrane purportedly practiced scales and other technical exercises for more than eight hours each day. However, Coltrane acknowledged that practicing without purpose is unproductive. One needs to understand *why* before understanding *how*.[11]

Planned continuity was discussed previously, and maintenance of culture would have to be partially achieved through planned continuity. "Just doing the same things in the same way" is not enough. Collaboration, autonomy, and delegated authority with a focus on the future are needed in the culture.[12] Therefore, the importance, as with many aspects for succession planning, is to have a future-oriented approach.

IT'S A SIGN ALRIGHT

Rick Moranis's character was awaiting a sign in the movie *Ghostbusters*, which was heralded by the explosion releasing the captured specters.[13] Well, such an outward sign is often not displayed to document a positive or negative culture, but there are many identifiable indicators. Leaders must be cognizant to recognize the signs that are indicators of positive and negative qualities for organizational culture and climate.

The "management by walking around" concept was discussed in Chapter 11, and doing so will permit a leader to gauge the climate of the organization.

Even indirect feedback is helpful to gauge the climate. Using Mahsa Alizadeh's assertion, satisfied employees will provide positive feedback to others and encourage individuals to join the organization in new capacities and positions.[14] Understanding how employees portray the organization to others outside of the organization is a key indicator. Some key indicators, positive and negative, are included in Figure 12.1. Use the information to calculate a baseline for the climate of the organization.

POLAR OPPOSITES

Although many of the items in the lists for Figure 12.1 are dichotomous, there are a few for which some positive and some negative tendencies are noticeable in the organizational culture. Perfect examples may exist within the pages of textbooks, but in reality, no organization has a perfect culture and no organization has a completely toxic culture. But in understanding that climate is the outward perception of the organizational culture, how individuals experience the daily functions matters greatly.[15]

Only Seeing the Worst in People

To examine several facets in greater detail, employee responses in organizations with negative cultures can become manifested in several different behaviors depending upon the situation. Frequent absenteeism is a common trend. Employees who "use" an allotment of personal time immediately or in substantial quantities is often a sign that employees are finding any excuse not to be present at work. The inverse may be true as well, as presenteeism becomes a problem when employees are fearful to take personal time even when ill or injured.[16]

The facets of a negative culture do not have to be major issues either. Harassment, discrimination, or extreme mismanagement are signs of severe indifference or worse, yet 30% of respondents to a nationwide business survey expected to experience one of those extreme examples in the near future.[17] Even signs of greater subtlety are indicators of problems as well. A lack of investment in people, inconsistency in accountability, unethical leadership, unrealistic high-pressure situations, and unclear stated values are signs of a negative culture.[18]

One of the most difficult aspects of a negative organizational culture is the inability of current individuals to recognize negative values and norms. Negative culture can be manifested in an overly competitive perception of "win at all costs." Plus, when the "ends justify the means," assumptions can be made that would otherwise not be made in a positive culture. Additionally,

Attributes of a Positive Culture

[ ] Collegial and caring attitude among employees
[ ] Individuals are willing to take risks
[ ] Individuals will openly share failures
[ ] Evidence of distributed leadership
[ ] Suggestions and recommendations are encouraged
[ ] Dedication and hard work is recognized for all
[ ] Individuals describe the organization positively
[ ] Individuals seek informal mentors
[ ] Individuals offer to serve as informal mentors
[ ] A number of individuals volunteer for additional functions
[ ] Autonomy and flexibility are granted, but results are expected, too
[ ] Talent is recognized and individuals are rewarded
[ ] Senior leaders frequently interact with all employees
[ ] Trust is evident in all facets
[ ] Individuals remain with the organization over time
[ ] Leaders discuss the future with employees
[ ] Development and training options are available

Attributes of a Negative Culture

[ ] Sense of isolation or lack of collaboration
[ ] Absenteeism (i.e., missing work) is common
[ ] Presenteeism (i.e., working when ill) is common
[ ] "Back stabbing" or "cutthroat" competition
[ ] Favoritism shown to some employees
[ ] Individuals rarely share feedback with supervisors
[ ] Individuals describe the organization negatively or do not provide any indication at all
[ ] Few individuals volunteer for any additional functions
[ ] Accountability is only a "gotcha" tool for those not in favor
[ ] Talented individuals leave frustrated and undervalued
[ ] Senior leaders are isolated from others
[ ] Trust is predominantly absent
[ ] Employee turnover is frequent
[ ] Aspirations are infrequently or never solicited
[ ] Rarely are developmental opportunities provided

[   ] Number Positive   [   ] Number Negative

Figure 12.1. Counterculture Revolution

in a negative culture, attempts at correcting negative behavior are often seen as a person "not being a team player," or who does not care about the organization "winning."[19] Ethical individuals will not remain in a position very long if there are negative pressures to conform.

Unfortunately, those pressures and general poor climate and culture can "bring out the worst in people." Individuals who are predisposed to negative behaviors have a far greater likelihood of engaging in negative behaviors, including violent tendencies, when situated in a setting with a poor organizational culture.[20] Depending upon the type of culture, the effect on deviant behavior is significant.[21]

Always Look on the Bright Side of Life

Douglas McGregor delineated between two diametrically opposed theories of management in his seminal treatise, *The Human Side of Enterprise,* in 1960,[22] and while individuals in several disciplines have used the basis of Theory X and Theory Y for more than 60 years, McGregor purportedly was frequently discouraged that his principles had quickly become overgeneralized and inflexible, as cited by Ed Schein in the foreword written for McGregor's posthumously published final book.[23]

One can only speculate whether McGregor would have eventually expanded beyond the two theories; however, one aspect is clear that the quality of the leader matters most.[24] Fortunately, other scholars have continued motivational studies in management. William Ouchi's Theory Z was a logical progression, and his focus on the well-being of employees has shown to increase morale, satisfaction, and stability. According to Ouchi, happy and productive employees need support;[25] creating the culture to support employees is the best method to ensure retention.

Leaders who ascribe to a Theory Y or Theory Z approach not only have greater dispositions for positive motivation but also understand the importance of culture. From a previous study pertaining to succession planning, an elementary assistant principal described that

> [culture] is what allows schools to not have a tremendous turnover from year to year, it is what allows schools to be able to provide a very well-rounded education to students, and provide them with an opportunity to be hopeful about their futures.[26]

The shared values, norms, and beliefs that comprise the culture must be outwardly demonstrated. The old adage "actions speak louder than words" is true with culture. Leaders then need to be cognizant of actions aligning with the culture. Unfortunately, nearly three-quarters of business survey respondents indicated that supervisors' actions directly contradicted the stated values of the organization,[27] which is sad because actions, time, and resources are all contributing factors to the culture and climate.

How the resources are allocated is an indication of the values held by those in an organization.[28] Communicating those values is also a prime concern for leaders. Trust was previously described as the "heartbeat" of succession planning,[29] and for appropriate reasons. In her doctoral dissertation, Kara Grasser addressed communications concerns in school districts. She specifically cited the interaction of relationships, trust, and communication. A stronger relationship leads to a greater likelihood that information was trusted by stakeholders.[30]

CONCLUDING THOUGHTS

The importance of culture, especially for retention, can be summarized in one word . . . relationships. Relationships are the foundation for organizational culture. The elementary golden rule of treating others how one wants to be treated is the foundation for creating a positive culture and climate. Work is needed not only to create a positive culture but also to sustain a positive culture.

While most school leaders will not be remembered with the likes of Washington or Lincoln, each has an impact on numerous students, which, over the course of a career, could be several thousand. Securing buy-in from others is needed for success at any level and often takes time. The Japanese principle of *kaizen*—change through small, incremental steps—is apropos. However, there has to be a clear focus on improvement, not just change for the sake of change.

Having a sense of the climate is vital. Using Mahsa Alizadeh's recommendation, satisfied employees will be one's best marketing tool. The perceptions of current employees can also be used as baseline information on areas to improve. No organization has a perfect or completely horrendous culture. There will always be areas of strength and areas to improve. The key is to identify both ends of the spectrum.

Although theories of motivation and management were only discussed briefly, understanding employee motivation is important to creating a positive organizational culture. Support is the crucial component to a healthy culture, and lack of support is the primary reason why individuals leave educational organizations and the profession itself. Culture matters for retaining employees. Now that all of the phases of quality succession planning have been discussed, in the next chapter, the focus will turn to implementing a plan.

CHAPTER REFERENCES

1. McCall, M. W., Jr. (1997). *High flyers: Developing the next generation of leaders*. Harvard Business School Press.
2. Attributed to Karen J. Leonardi, M.S., former principal of Spring Creek Elementary School.
3. Owens, R. G., & Valesky, T. C. (2022). *Organizational behavior in education: Leadership and school reform* (12th ed.). Pearson Education.
4. Lee, L. C. (2015). School performance trajectories and the challenges for principal succession. *Journal of Educational Administration, 53*(2), 262–286. https://doi.org/10.1108/JEA-12-2012-0139
5. *ibid.*—Owens & Valesky (2022)
6. Barry, M., & Wilkinson, A. (2016). Pro-social or pro-management? A critique of the conception of employee voice as a pro-social behaviour within organizational behaviour. *British Journal of Industrial Relations, 54*, 261–284.
7. Fullan, M. (2005). *Sustainable leadership*. Corwin Press.
8. Hargreaves, A., & Fink, D. (2006). *Sustainable leadership*. Jossey-Bass.
9. *ibid.*
10. *ibid.*—Owens & Valesky (2022)
11. Phelps, N. (2020, December 3). *7 Lessons on practicing music you can take from John Coltrane, the "athlete" of improvisation*. https://nathandavidphelps.medium.com/7-lessons-on-practicing-music-you-can-take-from-john-coltrane-the-athlete-of-improvisation-f296bb3a0915
12. Khalid, K., & Nawab, S. (2018). Employee participation and employee retention in view of compensation. *Sage Open, 8*(4), 1–17. https://doi.org/10.1177/2158244018810067
13. Reitman, I. (Director, Producer). (1984). *Ghostbusters* [Film]. Columbia Pictures.
14. Alizadeh, M. (2014). *Influential factors in international students' college choice of a rural, regional university* [Doctoral dissertation, Eastern Kentucky University]. Eastern Kentucky University Encompass Online Dissertations and Theses. https://encompass.eku.edu/etd/240
15. Hoy, W. K., & Miskel, C. G. (2012). *Educational administration: Theory, research, and practice* (9th ed.). McGraw-Hill.
16. Cowan, R. L. (2018). When workplace bullying and mobbing occur: The impact on organizations. In M. Duffy & D. C. Yamada (Eds.), *Workplace bullying and mobbing in the United States* (Volume 1, pp. 201–218). Praeger.
17. Clayton, S. J. (2019, December 5). 6 signs your corporate culture is a liability. *Harvard Business Review*. https://hbr.org/2019/12/6-signs-your-corporate-culture-is-a-liability
18. *ibid.*
19. Campbell, J. L., & Göritz, A. S. (2014). Culture corrupts! A qualitative study of organizational culture in corrupt organizations. *Journal of Business Ethics, 120*(3), 291–311. https://doi.org/10.1007/s10551-013-1665-7

20. Van Fleet, D. D., & Griffin, R. W. (2006). Dysfunctional organization culture: The role of leadership in motivating dysfunctional work behaviors. *Journal of Managerial Psychology*, *21*(8), 698–708. https://doi.org/10.1108/02683940610713244

21. Di Stefano, G., Scrima, F., & Parry, E. (2019). The effect of organizational culture on deviant behaviors in the workplace. *International Journal of Human Resource Management*, *30*(17), 2482–2503. https://doi.org/10.1080/09585192.2017.1326393

22. McGregor, D. (1960). *The human side of enterprise*. McGraw-Hill.

23. McGregor, D. (1967). *The professional manager*. McGraw-Hill.

24. *ibid.*—McGregor (1960)

25. Ouchi, W. G. (1981). *Theory Z: How American business can meet the Japanese challenge*. Avon Books.

26. Parfitt, C. M., & Romano, B. M. (2022). Assessing succession-planning processes: A case study for improvement. In L. L. Sabina (Ed.), *School administrator succession planning: Identifying high-impact practices, programs, and frameworks in P–12 schools* (pp. 187–206). Information Age Publishing.

27. *ibid.*—Clayton (2019)

28. *ibid.*—Owens & Valesky (2022)

29. Ragins, B. R. (2016). From the ordinary to the extraordinary: High-quality mentoring relationships at work. *Organizational Dynamics*, *45*(3), 228–244.

Zepeda, S. J., Bengtson, E., & Parylo, O. (2012). Examining the planning and management of principal succession. *Journal of Educational Administration*, *50*(2), 136–158. https://doi.org/10.1108/09578231211210512

30. Grasser, K. (2022). *Sensemaking and crisis communication: How school leaders communicate in times of crisis* (Publication No. 29168058) [Doctoral dissertation, George Washington University]. ProQuest Dissertations and Theses Global.

Chapter 13

Bringing a Plan to Fruition

Among scholarly sources, there is minimal practical information pertaining to executing a succession plan. A notable reason is the fact that every organization, every scenario, every plan is going to be different. Through the previous chapters, some practical advice was given, and the focus of this chapter is "to connect the dots" and bring everything together coherently. Regardless of the current organizational status, the goal is to be prepared.

ROTHWELL'S 15 CHARACTERISTICS

Before providing details by the major phases, a review of William Rothwell's 15 components[1] is needed, because many of those facets impact several phases. Although three major phases with an overarching concern for organizational culture has been the foundation of the chapters throughout this book, succession planning should be viewed as a continuous process. Depending upon current leadership needs, the focus may be needed on specific aspects and specific positions. For instance, if a long-serving associate superintendent for curriculum is planning on retiring in a few months, the need is different from one who just was promoted.

In review, Rothwell's characteristics are the following: (a) senior management participation, (b) benchmarking and needs assessment, (c) a developmental focus, (d) dedicated responsibility, (e) emphasis at all organizational levels, (f) a systematic approach, (g) analysis of future potential, (h) timeframe for replacement, (i) accountability to prepare successors, (j) specific training and development, (k) continual performance review of current employees, (l) understanding of the specific culture, (m) critical review of procedures, (n) focus beyond a next promotion, and (o) formal mentoring.[2]

While some of the characteristics are specific to a dedicated phase such as formal mentoring or training and development, others are overarching, including an all-level emphasis, participation of senior leaders, understanding of culture, and critical review of procedures. Therefore, viewing succession planning as a complete process is important for overall success. Although the concept had been previously mentioned, an important point is that a succession plan should not be viewed as "set in stone," and instead viewed as a continually evolving process.

CREATIVE BRAINSTORMING

Returning to concepts discussed earlier in the book, one must "know the destination before beginning the journey." Strategic plans; major initiatives; lists of job requirements, knowledge, skills, and dispositions; position descriptions; and assessment documents and rubrics are most likely needed. Even without those documents, an important consideration for planning is the focus on future needs, not just current ones.[3]

For a school district, some important considerations might be pertaining to the population. Is the population growing and new schools will need to be built, and therefore new principals prepared; or, is the population declining, and consolidations may need to be considered? Is student achievement improving, declining, or stagnant? What changes may be needed based on those and other "big picture" answers?

At a school level, the questions will be granular to a greater extent. Which teachers are best suited for leadership positions, as future principals, assistant principals, curriculum specialists, grade-level or subject/department chairs? Are there a sufficient number of individuals interested in leadership positions? Have those individuals received appropriate, future-oriented training and development? Are there quality mentors, and are individuals seeking others to serve as mentors?

PUT PEN TO PAPER

Once the requisite questions have been asked, and preliminary answers received, the actual plan needs to be drafted. Depending upon the answers, job and position descriptions may need to be written, initiatives may need to be created to align to a strategic plan, or even the strategic-planning process itself may need to begin. As with any major written project, several revisions will most likely be needed, and always with the mind-set that a quality plan must be flexible and fluid. With a goal of ensuring individuals are prepared for positions of greater authority at every level of the organization, craft the framework.[4]

Whether one describes the concept as a leadership pool, a pipeline,[5] or any other descriptor is inconsequential; what matters is having several individuals prepared for leadership positions at every level of the organization.[6] The next step after gathering preliminary documents and information is to identify the "lynchpin" positions and needed pools. Additionally, as Rothwell wrote, senior leaders need to be intimately involved throughout the entire process.[7]

The following are some questions to consider: "What does the ideal candidate look like for this job?" "What combination of education, training, experience, and skill set is needed for success now and in the future?" "What processes are in place to identify talent, and what processes are needed?" "After future leaders are identified, are there targeted and specific training opportunities available now?" "What changes need to be made to development and mentoring programs?" "Is the culture conducive to structured and informal mentoring?" "Are there effective retention efforts in place, and what efforts are needed?" These questions among many others need to be considered.

Please Identify

Embedded in those questions to consider are elements of the three major phases.[8] Writing the plan in a linear fashion could be helpful, and thus begin with talent identification. Using elements from the first few chapters of the book, from whom should leaders seek input? Are *all* appropriate stakeholder groups represented? Are the appropriate benchmarks in place to determine the knowledge, skills, and dispositions for candidates?[9] Whether internal or external, there will be challenges, so ensuring the proper cultural fit is vital.[10]

Frequent revisions and additions will be made, so aiming for perfection in a succession plan is a fallacy. Using Rothwell's characteristics[11] and involvement of appropriate individuals, such as human-resources personnel, will be instrumental in creating the first steps.[12] Once the identification components are drafted, a substantial amount of time will need to be devoted to creating the development and mentoring components.[13]

Aiming for the Correct Target

More so than at any stage of succession planning, development and mentoring must be considered with a future-oriented approach. School leaders, especially those at senior and executive levels, need to stay current with research trends. As a sign of wisdom, admitting what one does not know is important. But staying abreast of current research is important to address those knowledge gaps.[14] For example, Dawn Guice recently researched perceptions of school principals pertaining to the scope and depth of speech-language pathologists in a school setting and found that most lack a complete understanding pertaining to the role and function of speech-language pathologists.[15]

Learning about those widespread gaps are important; however, the development still must be targeted and specific.[16] Using Rothwell's assertion, development needs to be systematic and targeted for two steps in the future, not just the next promotion. Regardless of whether there are specific departments, offices, or personnel for leadership development, dedicated accountability is needed.[17]

Those responsible must ensure the developmental aspects are tailored specifically to the needs of the individual and coupled with the future needs of the organization.[18] Having and tracking written plans is an important component to do so. Analysis of needs is also going to be helpful. For instance, if a substantial number of aspiring principals have identified additional training to ensure they have the knowledge and skills to complete state-required reports correctly, then there is a great probability that current generic trainings are insufficient to meet the needs.

Even with specific developmental plans in place, 360-degree assessment of talent is needed. The opinions of those two levels above and below, peers, and external stakeholders are needed.[19] Because there are so many individuals, care must be taken to solicit appropriate information from all of the stakeholders, not just the "squeaky wheels." Being mindful of the concerns, Rothwell did caution that multirater assessments are time consuming and can be expensive, and should only be enacted if the organizational vision and direction is clear.[20]

While the answer is not always policies and procedures, having policies and procedures in place will be very beneficial for developmental aspects. Although the focus has not been overly stressed, having a completely transparent process will engender support from varying stakeholders, because the process and expectations are clear to everyone involved.[21] Additionally, a quality succession plan can be a tool to help leaders mitigate the political nature of leadership promotions and, in turn, help foster a positive organizational culture.[22]

Mentor and Protégé

As part of the positive organizational culture and as a subset of the developmental phase, ensuring formal and informal mentoring opportunities is crucial.[23] As was discussed in Chapter 9, no mentoring program will ever be perfect; therefore, addressing both facets is important. Having a high-quality structured mentoring program in place is needed, as well as fostering the conditions for individuals to serve as informal mentors and seek informal mentors.[24] Though a "program" for informal mentoring cannot be created nor mandated, the focus must be entirely on ensuring the positive organizational culture exists.

A positive culture is necessary for successful structured mentoring as well. In the "putting pen to paper" phase, senior leaders need to construct a mentoring program carefully, and have specific accountability to ensure a program is created and implemented with fidelity. The most successful examples of mentoring programs have several characteristics in common, including painstakingly matching protégés to mentors based on needs and personality factors.[25]

Above all else, trust is paramount. Previously described as the "heartbeat" of quality succession planning, trust is an individual and organizational characteristic needed for a positive culture and climate, and vital to true growth for a protégé.[26] Trust must be evident in both directions: a protégé must have trust in asking for help and simply saying, "I do not know"; and a mentor must provide a trusting environment for growth and creating the conditions in which the protégé is comfortable asking for help.

No plan or blueprints can be given for creating a culture of trust, but there are components that are within the purview of senior leaders when creating mentoring programs. One, ensure that any person who volunteers to serve as a mentor truly wishes to help others succeed and is not simply "volunteering" because a stipend or other benefit is involved.[27] Two, ensure the requirements and expectations are clear in advance, and provide a minimum threshold for acceptability. Three, provide opportunities for all participants to provide feedback for future programmatic improvements.

Retention, Retention, Retention

Although the final phase of quality succession planning is also the "wildcard" for the process, insight and care must be given, and data must be analyzed appropriately. The use of static and dynamic measures can only provide partial answers.[28] Because so many external factors beyond the control of senior leaders are involved, expecting every stellar employee to remain is not a logical goal. Despite the best efforts, some employees will always seek other opportunities. However, viewing the preparation of others for positions of greater responsibility as a moral imperative will lead to success.[29]

While knowing some individuals will eventually leave to seek opportunities with other organizations, tacitly approaching retention is not a prudent option. Knowing that lack of administrative support is the number one reason why individuals leave the education profession, steps must be taken to address concerns. But, for a succession plan, what are the appropriate initiatives to have for retention? There is never going to be a universal answer.

The model provided in Chapter 11 for increasing job content and responsibilities is an appropriate start.[30] Ultimately, senior leaders need to "have a finger on the pulse" of the organization and take active steps to ensure a positive culture and climate exist. Using Mahsa Alizadeh's assertion, leaders should want the type of culture in which employees are satisfied and engaged and in turn help recruit others to join.[31] So in essence, a quality focus on development and mentoring is also an effort for retention.

As a paradigm change in thinking, viewing talent as an organization-wide asset and considering the leadership pipeline at every level of the organization are needed for retention efforts.[32] Unlike traditional models of business planning in which the focus was limited to executive or senior level positions, the consideration for every level will require leaders to address the needs of the lowest-level employees. As an example of being familiar with the research, Amanda Rose's contention was that many school principals had expectations that were too great for new teachers with alternative certification.[33]

Only by knowing the needs of the organization can specific activities be written. Additionally, a focus on creating and maintaining a positive organizational culture and climate will be requisite in ensuring any initiatives are successful. As Brianne Lopez-Romano wrote in her doctoral dissertation, those leaders who were successful in turning around a failing school consciously focused on the organizational culture.[34]

REVISING THE DRAFT

Quality succession planning is a recursive process, and one for which many changes will be made. Despite the best level of planning and considerations, unexpected and unavoidable circumstances will arise. Once the plan is written, revisions should be made and clarifications considered, and then the revisions should be shared with all the appropriate stakeholders for feedback. One of the principles not addressed in as much depth is Rothwell's assertion for having a timeframe for replacement.[35]

The timeframe for seeking a new leader is before the position is vacant.[36] While educational entities do not generally have the budgets the same as for-profit businesses or large-scale organizations, lessons can be learned and applied with modification. For example, nursing researchers have recommended hiring a new manager a year prior to the retirement of the outgoing leader. Paying two salaries was more cost effective than having instability from an unplanned transition.[37] Part of the lesson is that when new information is learned, the plan must be adjusted accordingly.

Bringing a Plan to Fruition 125

CONCLUDING THOUGHTS

While "concrete" steps cannot be given because every setting, every organization, every situation will be different, the concepts proposed or reiterated in this chapter should help a leader begin the process of creating a quality succession plan. Using William Rothwell's 15 characteristics and a focus on the initiatives for identification, development and mentoring, and retention will provide a solid foundation.

Depending upon the level of detail written, a quality succession plan can easily exceed several hundred pages in length. To provide some guidance, an

---

Example Strategic Goals for Succession Plan Implementation

- Revise all job descriptions to align with future needs and secure approval from the school board.
- Implement a new HR system for advertisement, applications, screening, and onboarding.
- Add succession management discussions as a standing topic for executive-level leadership meetings.
- Create a leadership assessment center within HR.
- Revise the pool processes for curriculum specialists, assistant principals, principals, and central-office administrators.
- Institute targeted development programs for all individual currently enrolled and continue for those admitted into the leadership pools.
- Provide opportunities for leadership development beyond internships required for degree programs.
- Revise evaluation systems to include components for leadership development and components for future success.
- Implement 360-degree evaluation procedures for all leadership positions and aspiring leader processes.
- Assess retention aspects for the school district.
- Conduct climate studies for individual schools and central-office entities.

Figure 13.1. Assessing a Succession Plan

example of high-level strategic goals for a quality succession plan is included in Figure 13.1. Every setting and organization will be different, and these goals may be appropriate for many organizations and not applicable to others, or even be a "step backwards." Always base consideration for creating the plans on future organizational needs.

CHAPTER REFERENCES

1. Rothwell, W. J. (2005). *Effective succession planning: Ensuring leadership continuity and building talent from within* (3rd ed.). AMACOM.
2. *ibid.*
3. *ibid.*
4. Chavez, J. (2011). The case for succession planning. *Strategic Finance, 92*(8), 15–16.
5. Conger, J. A., & Fulmer, R. M. (2003). Developing your leadership pipeline. *Harvard Business Review, 81*(12), 76–84.
6. Beeson, J. (2000). Succession planning: Leading-edge practices: What the best companies are doing. *Across the Board, 37*(2), 38–41.
7. *ibid.*—Rothwell (2005)
8. *ibid.*—Chavez (2011)
9. Wilkerson, J. R., & Lang, W. S. (2007). *Assessing teacher dispositions: Five standards-based steps to valid measurement using the DAATS model.* Corwin Press.
10. Sabina, L. L., & Colwell, C. (2018). Challenges of principal succession: Examining the challenges of hiring internal vs. external candidates. *Athens Journal of Education, 5*(4), 375–396.
11. *ibid.*—Rothwell (2005)
12. Gurchiek, K. (2015, November 15). *Don't leave succession planning to chance.* Society for Human Resource Management. https://www.shrm.org/hrdisciplines/orgempdev/articles/pages/leadership-manyorganizations-fail-at-succession-planning.aspx
13. *ibid.*—Chavez (2011)
14. Kamtchum-Tatuoen, J., & Zafack, J. G. (2021). Keeping up with the medical literature: Why, how, and when? *Stroke, 52*(11), 746–748. https://doi.org/10.1161/STROKEAHA.121.036141
15. Guice, D. D. (2021). *School leader perceptions regarding the role of the school-based speech-language pathologists* [Doctoral dissertation, Louisiana Tech University]. Louisiana Tech University Digital Commons. https://digitalcommons.latech.edu/dissertations/913/
16. Beeson, J. (1998). Succession planning: Building the management corps. *Business Horizons, 41*(5), 61–66.
17. *ibid.*—Rothwell (2005)

18. Durden, P. C., Izquierdo, J., & Williams, J. L. (2008). Out of the ashes: Building leadership and sustainability amid the chaos. *AASA Journal of Scholarship and Practice*, *5*(3), 47–51.

19. *ibid.*—Beeson (1998)

20. *ibid.*—Rothwell (2005)

21. Meyer, M. J., Macmillan, R. B., & Northfield, S. (2009). Principal succession and its impact on teacher morale. *International Journal of Leadership in Education: Theory and Practice*, *12*(2), 171–185. https://doi.org/10.1080/13603120802449660

22. Parfitt, C. M. (2017). *Perceptions of succession planning in educational organizations: A mixed-method study of four Florida school districts* (Publication No. 10289333) [Doctoral dissertation, Florida Gulf Coast University]. ProQuest Dissertations and Theses Global.

23. *ibid.*—Chavez (2011)

24. Holt, D. T., Markova, G., Dhaenens, A. J., Marler, L. E., & Heilmann, S. G. (2016). Formal or informal mentoring: What drives employees to seek informal mentors? *Journal of Management Issues*, *28*(1–2), 67–82.

25. *ibid.*

26. Ragins, B. R. (2016). From the ordinary to the extraordinary: High-quality mentoring relationships at work. *Organizational Dynamics*, *45*(3), 228–244.

27. *ibid.*—Holt, Markova, Dhaenens, Marler, & Heilmann (2016)

28. Farley-Ripple, E. N., Solano, P. L., & McDuffie, M. J. (2012). Conceptual and methodological issues in research on school administrator career behavior. *Educational Researcher*, *41*(6), 220–229. https://doi.org/10.3102/0013189X12451774

29. Smeltzer, C. H. (2002). Succession planning. *Journal of Nursing Administration*, *32*(12), 615.

30. Cloutier, O., Felusiak, L., Hill, C., & Pemberton-Jones, E. J. (2015). The importance of developing strategies for employee retention. *Journal of Leadership, Accountability and Ethics*, *12*(2), 119–129.

31. Alizadeh, M. (2014). *Influential factors in international students' college choice of a rural, regional university* [Doctoral dissertation, Eastern Kentucky University]. Eastern Kentucky University Encompass Online Dissertations and Theses. https://encompass.eku.edu/etd/240

32. *ibid.*—Beeson (1998)
ibid.—Chavez (2011)
ibid.—Rothwell (2005)

33. Rose, A. L. (2019). *Supporting alternative certification teachers' professional development needs in Florida: Knowledge of K–12 school leaders* (Publication No. 13808049) [Doctoral dissertation, Florida Gulf Coast University]. ProQuest Dissertations and Theses Global.

34. Lopez-Romano, B. M. (2020). *Turnaround principals' practices in the southeastern United States: A case study* (Publication No. 28412619) [Doctoral dissertation, University of West Florida]. ProQuest Dissertations and Theses Global.

35. *ibid.*—Rothwell (2005)

36. Sverdlik, B. (2012). Who will be our nursing leaders in the future? The role of succession planning. *Journal of Nursing Administration*, *42*(7/8), 383–385. https://doi.org/10.1097/NNA.0b013e318261938b

37. Beglinger, J. E. (2013). Designing tomorrow: Creative and effective succession planning. *Journal of Nursing Administration*, *43*(10), 495–496. https://doi.org/10.1097/NNA.0b013e3182a3e85b

Chapter 14

Assessing a Plan

A quote often misattributed to Peter Drucker is that "if something cannot be measured then it cannot be improved."[1] Although misattributed and not entirely true, the quote is apropos, because the focus of this penultimate chapter will be assessing succession plans. A word of caution, though, is to avoid false measures. For instance, in his doctoral dissertation James Thomas interviewed a superintendent who stated that the school district had a successful approach to succession planning because vacancies for principal were all filled by internal candidates yet could not provide any evidence of an actual process producing results.[2]

Quality assessment is multifaceted, and appropriate measures of success are needed. But what are those measures? Unfortunately, many individuals familiar with Peter Drucker's work take the misattributed statement literally and, often to their detriment, ignore facets deemed unmeasurable. For example, judgment, wisdom, and ethics are vital components needed for leadership, yet the concepts are difficult to measure.[3] Difficulty in measurement does not equate to a lack of importance. Furthermore, as will be discussed in this chapter, measurement and assessment are not synonymous.

As was mentioned in Chapter 3, a mixed-methods approach is important to understand *what* and *why*. Also stated in the chapter was a reliance on the standards promulgated by the Joint Committee for Educational Evaluation, because every situation is unique, and the evaluation must be adaptable.[4] Therefore, some generic principles to assess talent identification, targeted development and mentoring, retention of high-performing employees, and culture and climate are provided in this chapter.

A few examples from a succession plan for fictional *International School Districts* are included in Figure 14.1. Throughout the chapter, questions will be provided to determine the appropriateness for the goals. As with any case study, only limited information can be provided; therefore, the purpose is to make a general determination: is this fictional organization "on the right track"? Using the information will help make the determination.

International School: Succession Plan Highlights

Identification Initiatives

- Request principals to provide names of aspiring leaders to HR by October 1st.
- Post job descriptions on the school district website.
- Disseminate survey to all administrators inquiring about their intentions for the next academic year.
- Revise assistant principal pool process to align with recent changes to the state certification requirements.

Developmental Initiatives

- Hold trainings for all principal pool candidates for budgeting processes.
- Create a mandatory training before authorizing anyone to serve as a mentor teacher or leader.
- Require all assistant principal and principal pool candidates to submit a portfolio addressing leadership readiness then update annually.
- Collect and analyze data for mentoring programs.

Retention Initiatives

- Conduct retention analysis and study inter-district movement by teachers and principals.
- Take steps to lower attribution to less than 10%.
- Prepare in advance for collective bargaining, especially for salary concerns.

Overarching Initiatives

- Conduct a district-wide climate study.
- Establish town hall style events to seek public input.
- Begin discussion with the school board for the direction of the next 5-year strategic plan.

Figure 14.1. Case Study: Making the Case

Before disaggregating the points from the fictional example, a few clarifications need to be made. Measurement and assessment are not synonymous terms. The act of measurement is simply ascribing numerical information quantitatively. Assessment is then taking information and making a value judgment.[5] For example, a man and woman are both 5 feet, 10 inches tall. The information is simply a measurement calculation. To take the next step and assess, at 5 feet, 10 inches tall, the man is considered average, while the woman is considered tall; yet both are the exact same height. For succession planning, value judgments are needed, not just measures.

ASSESSING TALENT IDENTIFICATION

Talent identification is an assessment process itself; therefore, making a determination about talent identification is an assessment of the effectiveness of the process. Unfortunately longitudinal data are needed for complete assessment of effectiveness. However, long-term effectiveness is not the only measure needed. Using John Beeson's assertion from the business literature, the true goal is not to train a singular replacement but, instead, to have a pool of qualified candidates prepared to assume positions of greater responsibility.[6]

Dividing the assessment into short, medium, and long term will be an appropriate method to review. As was written in the last chapter, a truly comprehensive plan could easily outnumber the total pages of this book, so the discussion for assessment has to be focused on overarching and large-scale components. Reviewing the report for progress (or lack of progress) for an individual aspiring to be an assistant principal is far too granular for overarching assessment purposes.

Short-term assessment for talent identification should focus on documentation and procedures. Are the job and position description accurate? Do they reflect the future needs of the organization? Are multiple stakeholders involved in interviews and assessment? Are the proper application and screening systems in place? Although replacement planning (i.e., having a singular person identified) has been an obsolete concept in the business world since the last century,[7] having the information for a replacement timeline is in alignment with best practices.[8]

Medium-term goals will be highly dependent upon the circumstances for the organization. For instance, if a vast number of principals are nearing retirement, and few qualified individuals are prepared to assume the roles, then the need will be different from a school district in which many of the principals are earlier in their careers and few retirements or departures are expected in the near future. A six-month to one-year timeframe is appropriate.

The long-term goals need to be focused on perpetuating a qualified pool of leadership candidates for every level of the organization. The goals should be less tactical and more strategic than short- and medium-term goals. Focusing on the systems processes and execution with fidelity will be needed.[9] In essence, ensuring the appropriate aspects such as senior leadership involvement, multirater assessments, and a future-oriented approach become part of the culture are among the long-term needs.[10]

ASSESSING TARGETED DEVELOPMENT AND MENTORING

Short-term goals for development should focus on baseline information. What development programs are in place? Are the programs targeted and specific? Are they effective in ensuring individuals are prepared for the intended positions? But also, what are the upcoming needs of the organization? Is the culture conducive for mentoring? Are there a sufficient number of qualified individuals to serve as formal mentors?

Once the baseline data have been established, then for medium-term goals the focus will need to be ensuring the processes and procedures are in place, creating individual development plans[11] and ensuring "stretch" assignments are among the needs.[12] Ensuring the 360-degree evaluations of talent is an appropriate medium-term goal as well,[13] as is reviewing the scope and focus of the mentoring programs. In assessing, the question to ask is this: do these initiatives ensure there are numerous qualified individuals prepared for positions of greater authority?

Just as with identification of talent, the long-term goals for development and mentoring should be focused on the "big picture." Evaluation data from medium-term goals should influence the long-term strategies. Longitudinal data are needed to show effectiveness of development and mentoring programs. While assessing the developmental aspects of the succession plan should be viewed as understanding the "heart," if individuals are not prepared, then the plan is worthless.

ASSESSING RETENTION EFFORTS

Retention analysis for short-term goals should be focused on collecting and analyzing static and dynamic retention data.[14] How long have individuals remained in positions, and how long have they remained with the organization? What movement is notable among internal position changes? The short-term focus for retention has to be answering the question of *what*. The medium-term goals must answer the question of *why*.

Why are individuals leaving the organization? Is there appropriate administrative support? Is pay a concern? Do employees recognize a connection between performance and rewards? Once vacant, are positions filled with a qualified individual within a reasonable timeframe? Finally, are the expectations commensurate with the position and in alignment with the job and position descriptions?

For long-term goals, are discussions about future aspirations part of the leadership culture?[15] Analysis of the connection between development and retention needs to be undertaken clearly, along with other strategic assessments. Some of the issues such as discrepancies in pay can be addressed through long-term initiatives that cannot be handled immediately. Especially for critical school-based leadership positions, are principals remaining for five or more years?[16] Depending upon those answers, what changes can be made to improve positive outcomes?

ASSESSING CULTURE AND CLIMATE

The focus on a positive organizational culture is vital across all the phases. Understanding the norms, values, and beliefs held by the individuals in the organization is a crucial skill for leaders.[17] The short-term goals must be centered on understanding the culture and climate. Whether an official climate study is conducted or reliance on observational data are used, having information from which to base decisions is important.

Medium-term goals should be focused on addressing negative issues in the culture. Remember that destructive practices are easy to enculturate and then are often perpetuated without others realizing,[18] although the method to bring about cultural change should often be focused on creating positive, not necessarily undoing negative. Using the concept of *kaizen*,[19] offering opportunities for all stakeholders to provide input, and creating a positive culture is a long and possibly slow process.

The long-term goals should contain a focus to ensure the appropriate aspects are enculturated, and then positive aspects are sustained. Michael Fullan discussed the importance of a leader having an exit plan from the first day and building a sustainable culture.[20] Ensuring that distributed leadership has become part of the culture is one of most poignant strategies for creating sustainability.[21]

Through all the discussions pertaining to organizational culture and climate, the key point is that every organization, every district, every school, every subgroup will be different. The needs will be different, the direction will be different, and the areas for improvement will be different. As was discussed earlier in the book, there is no panacea, but organizational culture is the closest to it.

ASSESSING INTERNATIONAL SCHOOL DISTRICT

Having provided some very general points to consider, a high-level analysis for the strategic goals for the fictional International School District can be conducted. Many details were intentionally left nebulous so the reader can frame the discussion through the lens of a school system with which he or she is most familiar. Without knowing the specific organizational culture and many circumstances, recommendations can only be speculative.

Of the identification initiatives, the request for names of aspiring leaders is a positive aspect; however, there are several points to improve. The implication is that each principal is responsible for identifying leadership talent, which is antithetical to best practices. Unless each principal takes intrinsic responsibility to solicit input from all the varying stakeholders, the identification component will be biased.

Posting job descriptions on a website is positive for transparency; however, there was no discussion of the job descriptions being reviewed nor aligned to future needs. In terms of future needs, surveying administrators about intentions for the next academic year is a positive medium-term goal, but it should be expanded to determine a timeline for replacement. Simply replacing is an insufficient goal, and the initiative to revise the assistant principal pool process to meet state-mandated requirements is important, but it presumably lacks the specificity for targeted development. Lastly, the stated initiatives are all short to medium term; long term is also needed.

A presumption can be made for the initiative pertaining to budgeting, yet the execution is most likely generic. While a number of principal candidates need to understand the budgeting process, is the development targeted and specific? It's the same with the mandatory training for mentors. Having minimum requirements are positive, but is there specification to ensure mentors meet the needs of the protégés?

Requiring all pool candidates to submit a portfolio addressing leadership readiness has potential. The question will be in the execution. Will there be a 360-degree assessment of talent, a focus on performance management,[22] and a dual recognition for future developmental needs—by the individual and others? Collecting and analyzing data for the mentoring program is an acceptable short-term goal. However, analysis of the data are needed before the next course of action can be planned.

The retention initiatives are fairly abstract. The retention analysis study is promising as written. If static and dynamic measures are used, the "what" questions can be answered.[23] Once those data are analyzed, the qualitative questions must then be asked. Reducing attrition to less than 10% is an appropriate medium-term strategic goal; however, specifics will be needed. Also, was 10% chosen for a reason, or just to match general industry standards?[24]

The collective bargaining initiative will need greater discussion. Concern for salary is clear, and pay is typically among the lower of the top 10 reasons why educators leave the field.[25] But what is the goal for collective bargaining? Does the mind-set include one of the habits promulgated by Steven Covey, to seek a "win-win" opportunity,[26] or is the inclusion merely an attempt to provide a rationale why the salary is not competitive and little can be done to address salary concerns?

The overarching initiatives are also very nebulous. A climate study is positive. The questions would reside pertaining to the scope of the study. Are all of the requisite stakeholders going to be included? It's the same with the town hall events. For what purpose are the events to be held? By the nature of hosting a town hall–style event, the scope is probably going to exceed succession planning, so keeping the agenda specific and ensuring the correct questions are asked to secure appropriate input will be important.

Strategic planning is also vastly exceeding the scope; in fact, the opposite is true: a succession plan should support the strategic plan. Arguably, components for a quality succession plan can be written concurrently with a strategic plan. Because the focus has to be on future needs for a strategic plan, a quality succession plan is then needed to ensure there are qualified individuals at every level of the organization prepared to meet those future needs.

CONCLUDING THOUGHTS

In this penultimate chapter, some generic guidance was provided on assessing a written plan. Determining the appropriateness for short-, medium-, and long-term initiatives is one of the keys to assessing that a succession plan is appropriate. Be sure assessments are appropriate and measuring what is being purported to be measured. Also, do not disregard aspects that are measurable to a lesser extent.

Although the concept was only briefly covered previously, understanding the difference between measurement and assessment is needed to determine effectiveness for a succession plan. Measurement is the act of ascribing quantitative information. Assessment is using data to make a value judgment. Judgments are definitely needed for analyzing components to a succession plan. Some questions from which to judge include the following: were initiatives successful, was a particular outcome achieved, and are there qualified people prepared to assume positions of greater responsibility?

Now that principles for identification of talent, targeted and specific development and mentoring, retention of high-performing employees, overarching organizational culture, tips for creating a plan, and assessing a plan have been discussed, the final chapter will contain a focus on thoughts and general recommendations. As has been stressed throughout the book, quality succession planning will be different for every organization, and no two succession plans will be the same.

CHAPTER REFERENCES

1. Zak, P. (2013, July 4). *Measurement myopia*. Drucker Institute. https://www.drucker.institute/thedx/measurement-myopia/

2. Thomas, J. G. (2011). *Exploring succession leadership training for continuity of leadership in selected K–12 school jurisdictions in Alberta* (Publication No. 3674163) [Doctoral dissertation, University of Phoenix]. ProQuest Dissertations and Theses Global.

3. Prusak, L. (2010, October 7). What can't be measured. *Harvard Business Review*. https://hbr.org/2010/10/what-cant-be-measured

4. Yarbrough, D. B., Shulha, L. M., Hopson, R. K., & Caruthers, F. A. (2011). *The program evaluation standards: A guide for evaluators and evaluation users* (3rd ed.). Sage Publications.

5. Popham, W. J. (2006). *Assessment for educational leaders*. Pearson/Allyn and Bacon.

6. Beeson, J. (1998). Succession planning: Building the management corps. *Business Horizons, 41*(5), 61–66.

7. ibid.

8. Rothwell, W. J. (2005). *Effective succession planning: Ensuring leadership continuity and building talent from within* (3rd ed.). AMACOM.

9. Conger, J. A., & Fulmer, R. M. (2003). Developing your leadership pipeline. *Harvard Business Review, 81*(12), 76–84.

10. *ibid.*—Rothwell (2005)

11. Durden, P. C., Izquierdo, J., & Williams, J. A. (2008). Out of the ashes: Building leadership and sustainability amid the chaos. *AASA Journal of Scholarship and Practice, 5*(3), 47–52.

12. Chavez, J. (2011). The case for succession planning. *Strategic Finance, 92*(8), 15–16.

13. *ibid.*—Beeson (1998)

14. Farley-Ripple, E. N., Solano, P. L., & McDuffie, M. J. (2012). Conceptual and methodological issues in research on school administrator career behavior. *Educational Researcher, 41*(6), 220–229. https://doi.org/10.3102/0013189X12451774

15. De Clercq, D. (2021). Getting nowhere, going elsewhere: The impact of perceived career compromises on turnover intentions. *Personnel Review*. Advance Online Publication. https://doi.org/10.1108/PR-08-2020-0603

16. Hargreaves, A. (2005). Leadership succession. *Educational Forum, 69*(2), 163–173. https://doi.org/10.1080/00131720508984680

17. Owens, R. G., & Valesky, T. C. (2022). *Organizational behavior in education: Leadership and school reform* (12th ed.). Pearson Education.

18. Shaw, J. B., Erickson, A., & Harvey, M. (2011). A method for measuring destructive leadership and identifying types of destructive leaders in organizations. *Leadership Quarterly, 22*(4), 575–590. https://doi.org/10.1016/j.leaqua.2011.05.001

19. *ibid.*—Owens & Valesky (2022)

20. Fullan, M. (2005). *Sustainable leadership*. Corwin Press.

21. ibid.—Hargreaves (2005)

22. *ibid.*—Rothwell (2005)

23. *ibid.*—Farley-Ripple, Solano, & McDuffie (2012)

24. DailyPay. (2021, April 10). What is the average employee retention rate by industry? [2021 update]. Author. https://www.dailypay.com/resource-center/blog/employee-retention-rate/

25. Chase, B. (2000). Show us the money. *NEA Today, 18*(7), 5.

Darling-Hammond, L. (2001). The challenge of staffing our schools. *Educational Leadership, 58*(8), 12–17.

Ingersoll, R. M. (2001). Teacher turnover and teacher shortages: An organizational analysis. *American Educational Research Journal, 38*(3), 499–534.

Newberry, M., & Alsopp, Y. (2017). Teacher attrition in the USA: The relational elements in a Utah case study. *Teachers and Teaching: Theory and Practice, 23*(8), 863–880. https://doi.org/10.1080/13540602.2017.1358705

26. Covey, S. (2004). *The 7 habits of highly effective people: Powerful lessons in personal change* (rev. ed.). Free Press.

Chapter 15

Final Thoughts

Throughout the previous chapters, identification of leadership talent, targeted and specific development and mentoring, retention of high-performing employees, consideration of culture, and creating and assessing a succession plan were discussed. This final chapter will contain an iteration of the salient points and recommendations for quality succession planning for any educational entity.

The principles are the same whether an organization serves 100 students or more than 100,000; the difference will be in the scope, approach, and execution of the initiatives. For instance, a large school district may be able to dedicate a specific individual or office with leadership development responsibilities and then assign no other major responsibilities. A small, rural school district probably cannot do so, and the responsibilities will all be handled by the superintendent. What matters is that some person has the responsibility for ensuring appropriate leadership development.[1]

THE BUCK STOPS HERE

The famous sign from the desk of President Harry S. Truman has often been heralded as an example of a poignant leadership slogan. The purpose of the sign was to refute the slang concept of "passing the buck" and avoiding responsibility.[2] Involvement of senior leadership is one of William Rothwell's 15 characteristics,[3] and inclusion of human-resources personnel in the succession planning process is important;[4] however, the focus has to "come from the top." The chief executive and the leader for the board must "be the greatest cheerleaders" for having a strong succession plan, which includes senior-level involvement.

One important point is that those individuals must "walk the walk." The focus cannot be superficial or hypocritical. Paradoxically, from a 2013 study of succession-planning practices in private institutions of higher education, fewer than one-quarter of institutions had any succession plan, none that did were comprehensive, and the members of the board showed minimal interest in engaging in succession planning, yet the members of the board viewed their primary focus to be the hiring and evaluation of the chief executive.[5]

For proper succession planning to thrive, the philosophy must become a part of the culture and be perpetuated. Effective modeling by the chief executive is needed. Among those discussions with other senior leaders, the chief executive must be intimately involved in the identification, development, and retention of promising leaders at all levels. During his tenure as CEO of General Electric, Jack Welch was involved in selection and evaluation of leaders from the "C-suite" of top executives down to mid-level managers.[6] Of importance, input must be provided by senior leaders, but the decision remains with the hiring official.

NAVIGATING THE WATERS

There is a "double-edged sword" to having intimate involvement by senior leaders . . . the possibility of introducing politically motivated bias. Unfortunately, transparency in the succession-planning process was rated lowly among educators.[7] The solution is to engage all stakeholders openly and follow the process with fidelity. An aspiring principal once said that "if that political game went away [because of proper succession planning], I think that would help." Subjectivity will always be a part of the decision and is just human nature, but by following a specific process and involving others, the effects can be mitigated.

While misattributed to Warren Bennis and Peter Drucker, the saying "management is doing things right, while leadership is doing the right things"[8] is apropos for succession planning. As a process, succession planning must be conducted in the proper way. To ensure the process is implemented with fidelity, all the leaders involved must make proper and ethical decisions.

There will absolutely be challenges, and many individuals will want "favors"; however, "to do the right things," one will need to ensure the succession-planning processes are executed faithfully and truly base decisions on the best interests of the organization and those served. Trust has been mentioned throughout the book, and when choosing executive and senior leaders, trust is paramount. In fact, trust is probably the single greatest factor to forecasting success in a relationship between a chief executive and the top subordinate. A lack of trust between the two is often outwardly reflected as trouble within an organization.[9]

Trust is vital, but regardless of the level of trust between leader and subordinate, if competence is not present, then trust does not matter. Returning to the focus in the early chapters, does the person have the experience and credentials along with the knowledge, skills, and dispositions to be successful?[10] In essence, as Morgan McCall wrote, does the person truly have "the right stuff?"[11]

A CONSCIOUS EFFORT

But having a leader or even several with the right stuff does not matter if there is not a continuous pipeline to ensure there are always several qualified individuals prepared to assume positions of greater responsibility at all levels of the organization.[12] Ensuring the pipeline exists and the leadership continuity "flows" must be a conscious effort on the part of the chief executive and senior leaders.

As new information is learned, succession plans need to be adjusted and modified. There is an old adage about the best laid plans. . . . Continually improving metrics for talent identification and ensuring there is appropriate alignment with future needs are necessary. Development is an ongoing facet; one never stops learning. Although mentoring relationships typically only span two years, the foundation, once established, can grow and change.[13]

STAY CURRENT AND REACH FOR THE HORIZON

Change is one of the constants in life; individual changes, relationship changes, organizational changes. So, to be prepared and meet the changes proactively, one must stay current with research and best practices. Replacement planning was once considered a best practice, but shifts in business requirements made the process obsolete.[14] Concepts and processes will inevitably evolve, and new information will be discovered. Even the very concept of succession planning has only existed for about 75 years.

The earliest known study pertaining to succession planning arose from the Research and Development Board, which was established by the National Security Act of 1947. The secretary of defense at the time, James Forrestal, appointed Norman Asbury to study executive personnel administration. In his review of 53 major corporations, Asbury found five common themes among those organizations: an analysis of the organization, processes for executive selection, a focus on development, systems for evaluating personnel, and inventory-control mechanisms[15]—in essence, identification, development, retention, and organizational culture.

Even though the themes identified by Asbury mirror later research, a lot has changed since 1947. As an analogy, even though cars today have the same number of wheels as the cars of the 1940s, a lot has changed with the engine, transmission, and even the materials with which the cars are built. Therefore, with that mind-set, leaders need to stay current with research to manage succession planning appropriately.

The scope of research and best practices should not just be limited to research pertaining to succession planning in education. Beyond some researchers who occasionally study a topic that is germane to succession planning or narrowly address a component, there are not many who address the process in a comprehensive manner. Lou Sabina, who graciously wrote the foreword for the book, is one of the few; his articles and book are great resources.[16]

Exploration of other leadership topics can provide insight for aspects of identification, development, retention, or organizational culture. Just a few of the examples shared in earlier chapters are resources worth reading. Whether it's Amanda Rose's study on support for teachers with alternative certification,[17] Brianne Lopez-Romano's study on turnaround leadership,[18] Dawn Guice's study on relationships with speech-language pathologists,[19] Kara Grasser's study on crisis communication,[20] or Mahsa Alizadeh's study on international students at rural universities,[21] there is valuable information to learn.

Additionally, some of the component and supportive aspects should be examined to a greater extent. Assessment of dispositions by Kyle LaPaglia[22] and the seminal works by Steve Lang and Judy Wilkerson are indispensable for addressing the intangible aspects of leadership "fit."[23] Of course, the classic textbook *Organizational Behavior in Education,* by the late Robert Owens and Thomas Valesky, is valuable for aspects for organizational culture.[24] Some yet unknown authors will inevitably add to the body of scholarly literature from which to learn. Therefore, an effective leader must always keep reading and learning.

ALL ABOUT THE STUDENTS

Although the concept was mentioned only briefly in Chapter 1, a principal has the second most substantive impact on student learning after the teacher.[25] While every child in every school deserves the highest-quality teacher and the highest-quality principal, there will always be covariables involved in the equation. With a focus on instructional leadership and ensuring the proper individuals with the knowledge, skills, dispositions, credentials, and experience are identified, trained and mentored, and retained in school leadership positions, the goal can be closer to being achieved.

In the culture of each organization, one overarching conceptual lens should be used, and one overarching question asked: "is this decision in the best interest of the students for whom I am responsible?" Assistant principals, principals, central-office administrators, superintendents, and virtually all positions within an educational organization exist to ensure students receive the highest-quality education. By ensuring there are new leaders prepared at every level to assume greater responsibility, then an appropriate focus on student learning can be perpetuated.

BACK TO THE FUTURE

A consistent theme throughout the book has been the focus on the future. Not everyone is equal in ability to identify future possibilities. To provide some clarification for future needs, one does not need to plan for flying cars, invent the next product to spark a new technological revolution, or solve the most difficult of adaptive problems. Future needs include an understanding of changing demographics, preparing for new societal trends and advances, and ensuring all of the students have the knowledge, skills, and dispositions to be successful in whatever endeavors they undertake in life.

To paraphrase John Adams, education must not exist for the few, but for the many, so that the nation can be prepared for the future.[26] Preparing students to be engaged citizens was an early purpose of public education and needs to remain so today. Teaching students "how to think, not what to think" is needed to ensure the next generation is prepared to meet the challenges of tomorrow, whatever they may be.

While there are plenty of sources claiming the current generation of students needs to be prepared for jobs that do not even exist yet, as shown in review of the most in-demand jobs for the next 10 years according to the Bureau of Labor Statistics, the greatest needs are found in the home health care industry, restaurant business, software development field, nursing, transportation services, business management, marketing, security, sanitation, and physical fitness fields.[27] These are jobs that have all existed for more than 20 years, and many for 100 or more years.

For comparative purposes, 25 years ago, the greatest needs were administrative and clerical support; service workers; operators, fabricators, and laborers; professional workers; and salesworkers. The projections for occupations in 2000 with the greatest need were technicians and related support workers; service workers; salesworkers; executive, administrative, and managerial workers; and professional workers.[28] While not an "apples-to-apples" comparison, from historical and recent data, the vast majority of students are not going to be employed in jobs that do not exist yet.

However, are the ways those jobs function the same as in the 2000s or the 1980s? No. Just as a succession plan needs to be future oriented with the focus on having qualified leaders at every level of an educational organization, the focus on preparing students has to be on having the knowledge, skills, and dispositions to be successful in any future occupation—the ones that exist today and the ones that truly do not exist yet, or exist in a way not yet imagined.

CONCLUDING THOUGHTS

Preparing students for the future requires future-oriented educators and educational leaders. While no two organizations or even entities within an organization will be the same, the framework for ensuring qualified leaders are prepared to assume positions of greater responsibility at every level of the organization is the same. Identify the most promising leadership candidates; provide future-oriented, targeted, and specific development and mentoring; and retain the highest-performing employees by actively focusing on the organizational culture.

While comprehensive succession planning must "come from the top," leaders at every level of an organization have a moral responsibility to prepare others for future leadership positions, even knowing that some will seek other opportunities. Using the information from the preceding pages, create a plan to fit the specific needs of the organization, whether it be a major school district, a small independent school, a vocational center, or even smaller entities within another, then continually amend the plan with new information, and always ensure there are well-prepared individuals ready to assume greater responsibility.

A successful succession plan is not written for today, but for tomorrow, the next month, the next year, and beyond. Because organizational culture is like glass—laborious to create but easily destroyed—once a succession plan is written and edited, the work of executive and senior leaders is not finished. The culture must continually be a focus, and new and promising leaders will need to be identified. Staying current on research and preparing those at all levels for the future and focusing on retaining qualified individuals are essential. Although there are costs and succession planning is a process without end, the continual results of having prepared leaders is priceless.

CHAPTER REFERENCES

1. Rothwell, W. J. (2005). *Effective succession planning: Ensuring leadership continuity and building talent from within* (3rd ed.). AMACOM.
2. Harry S. Truman Library and Museum. (n.d.). *"The buck stops here" desk sign.* Author. https://www.trumanlibrary.gov/education/trivia/buck-stops-here-sign
3. *ibid.*—Rothwell (2005)
4. Gurchiek, K. (2015, November 15). *Don't leave succession planning to chance.* Society for Human Resource Management. https://www.shrm.org/hrdisciplines/orgempdev/articles/pages/leadership-manyorganizations-fail-at-succession-planning.aspx
5. Klein, M. F., & Salk, R. J. (2013). Presidential succession planning: A qualitative study in private higher education. *Journal of Leadership and Organizational Studies, 20*(3) 335–345. https://doi.org/10.1177/1548051813483836
6. Tichy, N. M. (2014). *Succession: Mastering the make-or-break process of leadership transition.* Portfolio/Penguin.
7. Parfitt, C. M. (2017). *Perceptions of succession planning in educational organizations: A mixed-method study of four Florida school districts* (Publication No. 10289333) [Doctoral dissertation, Florida Gulf Coast University]. ProQuest Dissertations and Theses Global.
8. Drucker Institute. (n.d.). *Did Peter Drucker say that?* Author. https://www.drucker.institute/did-peter-drucker-say-that/
9. Bennett, N., & Miles, S. A. (2006, May). Second in command: The misunderstood role of the chief operating officer. *Harvard Business Review*, 71–78.
10. Parfitt, C. M., Rea, D. C., Carter, C. F., Wilkerson, J. R., Rose, A. L., & Valesky, T. C. (2019). Assessing leadership dispositions: Does explicit instruction matter? *Southeast Journal of Educational Administration, 19*(1), 67–77.
11. McCall, M. W., Jr. (1997). *High flyers: Developing the next generation of leaders.* Harvard Business School Press.
12. Conger, J. A., & Fulmer, R. M. (2003). Developing your leadership pipeline. *Harvard Business Review, 81*(12), 76–84.
13. Parfitt, C. M., & Rose, A. L. (2020). Informal mentoring for aspiring school leaders: A phenomenological study. *Mentoring and Tutoring: Partnership in Learning, 28*(3), 278–294. https://doi.org/10.1080/13611267.2020.1778837
14. Beeson, J. (1998). Succession planning: Building the management corps. *Business Horizons, 41*(5), 61–66.
15. Zaich, L. L. (1986). *Executive succession planning in select financial institutions* (Publication No. 8612669) [Doctoral dissertation, Pepperdine University]. ProQuest Dissertations and Theses Global.
16. Russell, J. L., & Sabina, L. L. (2014). Planning for principal succession: A conceptual framework for research and practice. *Journal of School Leadership, 24*(4), 599–634.

Sabina, L. L. (Ed.). (2022). *School administrator succession planning: Identifying high-impact practices, programs, and frameworks in P–12 schools.* Information Age Publishing.

Sabina, L. L., & Colwell, C. (2018). Challenges of principal succession: Examining the challenges of hiring internal vs. external candidates. *Athens Journal of Education, 5*(4), 375–396.

17. Rose, A. L. (2019). *Supporting alternative certification teachers' professional development needs in Florida: Knowledge of K–12 school leaders* (Publication No. 13808049) [Doctoral dissertation, Florida Gulf Coast University]. ProQuest Dissertations and Theses Global.

18. Lopez-Romano, B. M. (2020). *Turnaround principals' practices in the southeastern United States: A case study* (Publication No. 28412619) [Doctoral dissertation, University of West Florida]. ProQuest Dissertations and Theses Global.

19. Guice, D. D. (2021). *School leader perceptions regarding the role of the school-based speech-language pathologists* [Doctoral dissertation, Louisiana Tech University]. Louisiana Tech University Digital Commons. https://digitalcommons.latech.edu/dissertations/913/

20. Grasser, K. (2022). *Sensemaking and crisis communication: How school leaders communicate in times of crisis* (Publication No. 29168058) [Doctoral dissertation, George Washington University]. ProQuest Dissertations and Theses Global.

21. Alizadeh, M. (2014). *Influential factors in international students' college choice of a rural, regional university* [Doctoral dissertation, Eastern Kentucky University]. Eastern Kentucky University Encompass Online Dissertations and Theses. https://encompass.eku.edu/etd/240

22. LaPaglia, K. (2020). *Preservice teacher dispositions: A case study of changes during a teacher preparation program* (Publication No. 28314521) [Doctoral dissertation, Florida Gulf Coast University]. ProQuest Dissertations and Theses Global.

23. Wilkerson, J. R., & Lang, W. S. (2007). *Assessing teacher dispositions: Five standards-based steps to valid measurement using the DAATS model*. Corwin Press.

24. Owens, R. G., & Valesky, T. C. (2022). *Organizational behavior in education: Leadership and school reform* (12th ed.). Pearson Education.

25. Marzano, R. J., Waters, T., & McNulty, B. A. (2005). *School leadership that works: From research to results*. Association for Supervision and Curriculum Development.

26. University of Virginia. (n.d.). *John Adams to Matthew Robinson Jr.: 23 Mar. 1786*. Founders Early Access. https://rotunda.upress.virginia.edu/founders/FOEA-03-01-02-0563

27. U.S. Bureau of Labor Statistics. (2021). *Occupational outlook handbook: Most new jobs*. https://www.bls.gov/ooh/most-new-jobs.htm

28. Silvestri, G. T., & Lukasiewicz, J. M. (1987, September). Projections 2000: A look at occupational employment trends to the year 2000. *Monthly Labor Review*, 46–63. https://www.bls.gov/opub/mlr/1987/09/art5full.pdf

Index

Adams, John, 143
administrative support, 94, 99, 106, 123, 133
Alexander the Great, 109
Alizadeh, Mahsa, 103, 112, 115, 123, 142
analysis of written plans, 122
Asbury, Norman, 141
assessment: 360-degree, 13, 18–19, 27, 29, 34–36, 66, 122, 132, 134; avoiding subjective, 11, 13, 66, 104; cross-functional, 19, 104; definition of, 129, 131, 135; dividing into short-, medium-, and long-term, 131; formative, 6; multifaceted, 76, 129; of dispositions, 17, 43, 46, 77, 142
aspirations, 94, 103, 133
autonomy, 94, 103–104, 111
avoiding responsibility, 139

baseline data, 132
Beeson, John, 1, 34, 36, 46, 131
Bennis, Warren, 140
best practices, 1, 6; lack of understanding, 11, 18–19, 35, 61, 92, 134; use of, 131, 134, 142
Bridges, Edwin, 25
Brittingham, Sharon L., 57
Bureau of Labor Statistics, 143

Caesar, Julius, 109
Carroll, Lewis, 15
Carter, Cecil F., 76
certification: needs of those with alternative, 4, 124, 142; requirements for, 48, 56, 61
change agents, 15
Chavez, Jodi, 16
Churchill, Winston S., 109
classroom-based training, 56, 65
"cleaning up a mess," 35
climate study, 102, 105, 133. *See also* organizational culture and climate
collaborative partnerships, 48
Collins, Jim, 90
Colwell, Chris, 35, 37
commensurate (appropriate) experience, 48–49, 54
Conger, Jay, 18, 33
Covey, Steven, 135
Crenshaw, Jeannette, 37
culture. *See* organizational culture and climate

decision-making processes, 25–26, 38
dedicated responsibility, 2, 64–65, 67, 73, 76, 119, 122
destructive leadership practices, 15, 18, 37, 133

dispositions: definition of, 16; improvement of, 77, 141; morality versus standards-based, 43. *See also* assessment; knowledge, skills, and dispositions
distributed leadership, 37, 46, 111, 133
Drucker, Peter F., 29, 129, 140
Durden, Phyllis, 55

employee loyalty, 103
enculturation, 65, 71–73, 77, 81, 111
engaged citizens, 143
executive/senior-level involvement, 66, 73, 132, 139–140
"exit plan," 28, 133

Fink, Dean, 4
fiscal responsibility, 64
formal mentoring, *See* structured mentoring
former colleagues: supervision of, 37, 72
Forrestal, James, 141
Fullan, Michael, 4, 28, 37, 65, 133
Fuller, R. Buckminster, 62
Fulmer, Robert, 18, 33
future: identification of needs, 55, 57, 66, 72–74, 120, 122, 131, 134–135, 141, 143; suitability, 28, 31, 34, 49, 54

Gandhi, Mahatma, 109
generic training: avoidance of, 55, 61, 67, 74, 122; definition of, 61
Grasser, Kara, 115, 142
Griffith, Mary B., 34
Guice, Dawn D., 121, 142

Hargreaves, Andy, 4, 36
Henry, Misty L., 15
high-quality talent characteristics, 16

identification of talent, 3, 11, 14, 25, 29, 36, 49, 83; consideration of culture in, 14; definition of, 11; internal versus external, 33
ill-defined roles, 93
indirect costs, 78, 91, 96
individual development plan, 34, 55
informal mentoring: as part of the culture, 57–58, 82, 121–122; benefits of, 57, 84–85; challenges with, 84; definition of, 83
instability causing turnover, 36, 92
insufficient planning, 92
Interstate School Leaders Licensure Consortium, 17
internal versus external talent, 17–18, 33–34
Izquierdo, Jorge, 55

job, task, and position analysis, 28, 120
John Paul II, Saint, 109
Joint Committee for Educational Evaluation, 127, 129
Jones, John R., 15

Kaizen, 64, 111, 115, 133
Klein, Melissa, 62
King, Martin Luther, Jr., 109
knowledge, skills, and dispositions, 11, 15–18, 20, 28, 33, 35, 43, 46, 49, 56, 65, 71, 74, 77–78, 120–121, 141–144; assessment of, 43, 77; importance of, 43, 143

lack of appreciation, 93
lack of support, 37, 71, 94, 99, 115
laissez-faire approach, 110
Lang, W. Steve, 16, 46, 142
Lao Tzu, 109
LaPaglia, Kyle, 46, 142
leadership development, 20, 54, 61, 64–65, 67, 73–74, 77
learning curve, 34, 102
Lee, Linda C., 5, 34, 38, 77
Lincoln, Abraham, 109, 115
Lopez-Romano, Brianne M., 36, 124, 142

loss of talent from greater marketability, 56

management compared to leadership, 140
"Management by Walking Around," 102, 106, 111
Marshall, Catherine, 26–27
Marzano, Robert J., 5
McCall, Morgan W., Jr., 3, 16, 48, 53, 109, 141
McGregor, Douglas, 114
McNulty, Brian A., 5
measurement: compared to evaluation and assessment, 129, 131, 135; difficulty in, 129
mentoring: components of, 56–58, 81–82, 122–123; definition of, 81–82. *See also* informal mentorying; structured mentoring;
minimum requirements: need to exceed, 134; no deviation from, 47
Moranis, Rick, 111
multiple measures of talent: definition of, 18; for interviews, 34; need for, 25, 35; problems with, 31

organizational culture and climate: definition of, 3, 110; importance of, 2–3, 5, 14, 16, 29, 33–34, 37–38, 48–49, 57, 67, 78, 82, 91, 99, 102–103, 109–110, 133–134, 142; perpetuating, 35, 64–65, 72, 83–84, 110, 124, 144; positive and negative aspects, 34, 46, 47, 90, 105–106, 111, 114–115, 122
Ouchi, William, 114
overlapping tenure, 124
Owens, Robert G., 3, 25, 110, 142

Packard, David, 102
Patton, George S., 109
pay gap (concern for salary), 93, 99, 102, 135
performance management, 3; 36, 76

pipeline of talent, 18, 33, 66, 104, 120–121, 124, 141
planned continuity/discontinuity, 5, 34–35, 38, 77, 111
Player, Gary, 20
policies and procedures, 122
politics, avoidance of, 66
pool of talent, 5–6, 8, 34, 46, 91–92, 120–121, 131–132
portfolio, 76, 134
potential, 6, 16, 19, 28, 33, 53, 119
preparing successors, moral imperative to, 34, 54, 123
problem diagnosis, 101
professional judgement, 33, 72
Professional Standards for Educational Leaders, 17
Program Evaluation Standards, 27
"putting out fires," 29

rapid turnover, 1, 4–5, 35
recursive process, 6, 104, 106, 124
replacement planning, 1, 131, 141
replacement timeframe, 2, 55, 119, 124
research, stay current with, 121, 141–142
Research and Development Board, 141
resource allocation, 62, 115
retention: benefits of, 64, 71, 78, 90, 114; definition of, 89; dynamic, 89, 123, 132; effect of culture on, 36, 93, 95, 99, 103–104, 106, 109, 115, 124, 133; industry standard, 135; static, 89, 123, 132
rewards, 93
Riddick, Francine P., 1
"Right stuff" theory, 3, 16, 48, 53, 109, 141
role ambiguity, 74
role conflict, 72–74
Rose, Amanda L., 4, 124, 142
Rossman, Gretchen B., 26–27
Rothwell, William J., 2–3, 18, 20, 27, 33, 36, 65–66, 76, 94, 119, 121–122, 124–125, 139

Sabina, Lou L., ix–x, 35, 37, 142
Salk, Raintry, 62
saturation, 26–27
Schein, Ed, 114
Stake, Robert E., 27
strategic planning, 120, 135
"stretch" or special assignments, 20, 34, 75, 85, 132
structured (formal) mentoring: benefits of, 82–83; challenges with, 83; definition of, 82
succession planning: characteristics of, 3, 14, 19, 25, 28, 34, 46, 53, 64–65, 72, 81–82, 104, 111, 119, 124, 136, 141; definition of, 2–3; phases of, 2, 11, 20, 89, 123
sustainability, 4–5, 37, 111, 133

talent appraisal, 3, 28
talent management, 53, 81, 103–104
targeted development, 55–56, 61, 71, 104, 129, 132; characteristics of, 56; definition of, 54; dual focus, 71–73; example framework, 104

tests of expertise, relevance, and jurisdiction, 25
Thatcher, Margaret, 109
Theory X and Theory Y, Chapter 12, 114
Theory Z, 114
Thomas, James, 129
Tichy, Noel, 56, 66, 76
transparency, 28, 64, 67, 134, 140
Trepanier, Sylvain, 37
Truman, Harry S., 139
trust, 36, 46–47, 57, 81, 83–85, 104, 115, 123, 140
turnaround leadership, 4, 35–36, 142

Valesky, Thomas C., 3, 25, 76, 110, 142

Washington, George, 109
Waters, Timothy, 5
Welch, Jack, 29, 54, 140
Wilkerson, Judy R., 16, 46, 142
Williams, James, 55

About the Author

Christopher M. Parfitt, EdD, is the senior director of grants and alumni relations at Hodges University. He earned his terminal degree from Florida Gulf Coast University and holds degrees from Seton Hill University and the University of Pittsburgh. Parfitt is past president of the Southern Regional Council on Educational Administration and coeditor of the *Southeast Journal of Educational Administration*. He has served as director of institutional effectiveness, coordinator of program assessment, and assistant professor of educational leadership. Prior to service in academia, he held school leadership, central-office, and teaching positions. His research interests also include dispositions of leadership candidates and collaborative partnerships.

www.ingramcontent.com/pod-product-compliance
Lightning Source LLC
Chambersburg PA
CBHW032215230426
43672CB00011B/2568